In Pursuit of The Trivial

Elaine

you look fantastic!

Thank you for reading this

Grahame

In Pursuit of The Trivial

a book about nothing

GIANFRANCO CUZZIOL

Published by Trivial Publishing

A CIP catalogue record for this book is available from the British Library.

ISBN 978-1-0686368-0-6

Book layout by Clare Brayshaw

Prepared and printed by:

York Publishing Services Ltd
64 Hallfield Road
Layerthorpe
York YO31 7ZQ

Tel: 01904 431213

Website: www.yps-publishing.co.uk

To Nonno and Nonna who sacrificed so much for me.

To my wife, Charlotte who has put up with me for so long.

To my daughters, Madalena and Beatrice who bring joy
and inspiration to my every day.

Thank you.

Contents

Opening

'I warn you that what you're starting to read is full of loose ends and unanswered questions. It will not be neatly tied up at the end, everything resolved and satisfactorily explained. Not by me it won't, anyway. Because I can't say I really know exactly what happened, or why or just how it began, how it ended, or if it has ended; and I've been right in the thick of it. Now if you don't like that kind of story, I'm sorry, and you'd better not read it. All I can do is tell what I know.'

Miles

The Body Snatchers by Jack Finney, 1955

Disclaimer

Flip-flop Clause

I reserve the right to have changed my mind by the end of this book or even perspective by perspective.

What seemed like a groundbreaking idea at the start might, by the end, just be me craving a coffee break.

Viewer discretion is advised for any sudden opinion reversals!

Animal Welfare Assurance

No animals, mythical or otherwise, were harmed, bothered, or even mildly inconvenienced in the writing of this book.

They've had a rather peaceful day, actually.

Nutty Disclaimer

While this publication is 100% nut free for your intellectual consumption, the author may or may not have indulged in a peanut butter sandwich during its creation. Allergic to ideas? EpiPens at the ready!

Success Attribution

Should you find wild success after using the material presented, remember it's all thanks to me.

You're welcome!

Failure Blame Game

On the flip side, any failures, misfortunes or general life mishaps after reading this book are entirely your own fault. It's probably due to misinterpreting my clearly genius material. Better luck next time!

Terms & Conditions Apply

Standard stuff, really. Don't read this while operating heavy machinery and always consult a professional before making life-changing decisions based on my ideas.

Why This Book ?

With a name like Gianfranco Cuzziol let me apologise in advance as you might expect me to look (see obligatory PR photo)[1] slightly more Italian. If I ever get the pleasure of meeting you (if I haven't had that pleasure already), you'll notice that I don't particularly sound or behave like an Italian. (The day I stopped eating pizza tells the tale of when I discovered I was less Italian than I thought.) But I am indeed the collaboration of a Venetian father and Neapolitan mother (to both of whom I am eternally grateful, amongst many other things, for meeting in Yorkshire, England). If you know anything of the Italian psyche then you might be aware that northern and southern Italians do indeed look and behave differently. I am a combination of a northern Italian exterior (reserved, calm, and often seemingly uninterested) but inside a southern Italian (chaotic, emotional, with a tendency to have piques of anger). More on stereotypes in marketing later.

Combine these traits with the fact that my parents actually raised me in Yorkshire then that might start to explain my slightly confused outlook and mindset. The importance of mindset in my line of work we discuss later as well.

So what is my 'line of work'? Well with a first degree in Astrophysics it will be of no surprise to you that I have spent most of my career in CRM (Customer Relationship Management) (a term that I detest), Data, Loyalty and Technology.

As a failed Astrophysicist, however, I can state with some confidence that most of what I have done in that career of 20 plus years is not rocket science. You can trust me on that.

With some conviction I can also claim to be one of the worst astrophysicists to have come out of the University of

---

1   https://cuzziol.com

Birmingham. So, I must now confess that my first job out of university was as a second-hand[2] car salesman, so I might have lost some of that trust. But that job gave me some insight into human behaviour that has stuck with me. Many potential car buyers would, of course, arrive in the car that they were thinking of trading in or part-exchanging. I would, of course, be duty bound to inspect the car and give them a 'reasonable' offer. After a cursory look at the paintwork, I would make a beeline for the boot. Its state was a clear pointer as to the owner's intent. If it was clear of clutter and had been hoovered, they had obviously invested time in getting it that way. They wanted to sell. If the trunk was as cluttered as mine, I regarded them as a potential time waster and gave them the least amount of attention. You could argue that today that is what we term Behavioural Targeting, based on an understanding of customer mindset. Understanding a customer's intent would seem an important consideration. With all that in mind, I was still a pretty bad salesman.

In essence, that's what this book is all about. It's a book about nothing (Matt Chokshi, I'm sure you will appreciate the Seinfeld reference here). It's a book about how I present my thoughts around CRM and Personalisation in a way that makes me smile and seemingly others as well. So, I thought, why not get it into print and then I can call myself an author as well!

But a book about nothing?

Everybody wants to write a book about something, so I took my inspiration here from one of my favourite TV shows, *Seinfeld*.

In the episode 'The Pitch' from season 4, George and Jerry pitch an idea for a show about 'nothing' to NBC executives.

---

2   I know these days we prefer preloved, but I can assure you some of these cars had never been shown any love.

The conversation in which George first proposes the concept to Jerry happens at Monk's Café, and can be summarised as follows:

George arrives at the diner with a burst of enthusiasm and tells Jerry that he has an idea for their pitch to NBC. When Jerry prompts him to share it, George excitedly explains the concept: a show about nothing. Confused, Jerry asks him to elaborate.

George proceeds to argue that most people's day-to-day lives don't consist of interesting stories or thrilling adventures but are instead filled with small, mundane and seemingly trivial events. He suggests that their show could focus on these everyday occurrences, portraying them in a humorous and entertaining way.

Initially sceptical, Jerry asks George what the content of the show would be, to which George emphatically responds: 'Nothing!' He goes on to explain that they can create comedy from these seemingly insignificant daily events – like waiting in line, buying a loaf of bread or going to the laundromat. He argues passionately that these mundane moments are something that everyone can relate to and would therefore make their show appealing to a broad audience.

Jerry seems doubtful about the idea, but he's intrigued by its novelty. He questions the feasibility of the concept but, after some consideration, ultimately agrees to give it a try, marking the beginning of the 'show about nothing'.[3] In the end, Seinfeld ran for nine seasons and one hundred and eighty episodes.[4]

---

3   https://www.youtube.com/watch?v=tSEEInFN_bY
4   https://en.wikipedia.org/wiki/List_of_Seinfeld_episodes

They do often suffer from 'imposter syndrome' and can't imagine NBC wanting to pay for this. Believe me, I've also had to convince myself that two thousand[5] people will buy this book.

This book is about nothing in particular, just examples of where I have had experiences in crafting my trade in the world of CRM, Loyalty and Personalisation. I try to stay clear of statistics pulled together by tech platforms (which of course only produce reports and white papers that support their product). My thoughts have, of course, been shaped by conversations I have had over my career, but I'll try to avoid filling the book with other people's thoughts and ideas.

The book design itself was inspired by the 'Newton, after William Blake' sculpture by Eduardo Paolozzi, outside the British Library. The bronze statue is a depiction of Sir Isaac Newton, as seen through the interpretative lens of William Blake, an English poet, painter, and printmaker, in his 1795 print 'Newton: Personification of Man Limited by Reason'. The print shows Newton leaning over with a compass at his feet, symbolising his scientific method. Blake, however, was critical of this empirical approach, believing it narrowed human understanding to a purely materialistic perspective, thus undermining our perception of spiritual and imaginative facets of life.

Paolozzi's sculpture brings this artwork to life. His statue presents Newton as a naked, muscular, crouched figure, focused on the mathematical calculations he is etching into the ground with a compass, oblivious to the beauty of the cosmos around him.

---

5   An arbitrary figure I've set myself.

That juxtaposition between art or nature and science has been my inspiration for the way I like to discuss the everyday aspects of my career to date. Eduardo Paolozzi, a Scottish artist, was born in Edinburgh in 1924, to Italian parents, another nod to my heritage.

The cover design was the work of Liz Williams[6] with whom I had the pleasure of working while CRM Director of the London-based agency, Zone.

Combining all this with storytelling as an age-old method of reinforcing a key message, I've come up with this book.

I hope you enjoy reading it as much as I enjoyed writing it.

Gianfranco

---

6   https://lizwilliams.uk/

Why are Basketball Players Tall?

Disclaimer: I am not, by any stretch of the imagination, a basketball fanatic or expert. *I think I may have played it on several occasions at school but that was many, many moons ago and I did marvel at the entertainment offered by the Harlem Globetrotters when they visited the UK once.*

In the realm of behaviour, understanding alone may not suffice; the true aspiration of marketers lies in effecting change.

Let's talk about Doctor James Naismith, the man who 'created' basketball.

To truly understand the brilliance of James Naismith and his creation of basketball, we must delve into his earlier experiences and the path that led him to the hallowed grounds of Springfield College. Naismith's journey began long before a fateful day in December 1891.

Born in 1861 in Ramsay Township, Ontario, Canada, Naismith was raised in a modest household that emphasised the values of education and physical activity. From a young age he exhibited a natural curiosity and an innate ability to observe the world around him. These qualities would shape his future endeavours and innovative thinking.

After completing his high school education, Naismith pursued his passion for knowledge at McGill University in Montreal. He excelled academically,

Dr James Naismith

earning degrees in physical education and theology. It was during this time that he developed a deep appreciation for the importance of physical fitness and the impact it had on the overall well-being of individuals.

Inspired by the teachings of Thomas Arnold, the renowned headmaster of Rugby School in England, Naismith became a staunch advocate of the holistic approach to education, which integrated physical activity into the curriculum. This belief laid the foundation for his future work as a physical education instructor.

Naismith's journey continued as he ventured to the United States to further his studies. He enrolled at the International YMCA Training School in Springfield, Massachusetts, where he encountered the challenging task of conditioning young athletes during inclement weather. It was within the confines of this training school that Naismith's creativity and problem-solving skills came to the forefront.

Driven by a desire to find a solution, Naismith stumbled onto a mission to invent a new game that could be played indoors, engaging both the mind and the body of his students. Little did he know that this audacious endeavour would forever change the landscape of sports and captivate the hearts of millions worldwide.

Naismith's unique blend of intellectual curiosity, passion for physical activity and unwavering determination culminated in the creation of basketball – a game that transcended boundaries and transformed the way people interacted on the court. His innovative thinking and ability to adapt to challenging circumstances set him apart as a visionary, forever etching his name in the annals of sports history.

His pre-Springfield years laid the groundwork for his pioneering work, providing him with the knowledge, experiences and mindset necessary to conceive a game that would inspire generations to come. His story serves as a testament to the power of human ingenuity and the profound impact one individual can have on the world through their innovative spirit.

Consider the scene. It's 1891, Springfield, Massachusetts, and Naismith, the physical education instructor, faced a conundrum. More precisely, it's December 1891 and it's bloody cold. So cold that the inclement weather prohibited outdoor training for his young athletes. Luckily, the YMCA International Training School possessed an indoor training facility – the gymnasium.

Equipped with football-shaped balls (or soccer-shaped balls as described by my North America acquaintances) and fruit baskets (peach, I believe), Naismith divided his 18 students into two teams, of nine I guess! The objective? Place the ball into the basket and earn a point. That seemed a tad too easy so to heighten the challenge, Naismith enlisted the janitor's (a Mr Stubbins) aid to attach the baskets to the lower rail of the gymnasium balcony, at a height of 10 feet – a measure you might recognise as being the height of today's 'hoop'. Okay, perhaps you now already know why basketball players are tall but bear with me a little longer.

A vexing problem emerged. Each time a point was scored, the game was halted, demanding the janitor's retrieval of the ball using a ladder. Consequently, Naismith asked the janitor to have the bottoms of the fruit baskets removed. Nonetheless, Naismith's vision did not unfold as anticipated, as skirmishes erupted amidst the game. Reflecting on this, Naismith later lamented, 'That was my big mistake. The boys began tackling, kicking and punching in the clinches. They ended up in a free-for-all in the middle of the gym floor. Before I could pull them apart, one boy was knocked out, several of them had black eyes, and one had a dislocated shoulder. It certainly was murder.'

Thus, Naismith outlined the original 13 rules of the game. And its name? 'Basketball,' Naismith proposed, dismissing the notion of calling it the 'Naismith Game'. Surely a stroke of genius!

From a design standpoint, the height of the original fruit basket inadvertently shaped the type of individuals who excelled in basketball. Over time, players grew progressively taller, gravitating near the basket, with the tallest players achieving success through 'dunks'. The graph below illustrates this trend, peaking around the mid-1980s, with an average player height of 6' 7" (201.2cm).[7]

Therefore, it becomes clear that basketball players are generally tall. Although you knew that anyway.

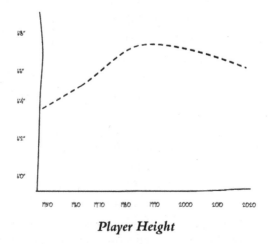

Player Height

7   Sourced from https://thehoopsgeek.com

However, a curious observation emerges from the graph. Since the mid–1980s, players have ceased growing taller and, to some extent, appear slightly shorter.

In 2023 I presented this at 30 conferences and not one person could tell me why this was. (In all fairness, I was sussed by an American basketball fan at my first conference in 2024.)

Examining the evident evolution of the game since 1891, there have been numerous rule changes, some major some less so. We note the addition of court lines, the presence of five players per team, a duration split over four quarters, time outs, and so on. Notably, the introduction of the 2–point rule occurred swiftly, while the inception of the 3–point shot took place around 1980. This was intended to serve as basketball's equivalent of baseball's home run but also aimed at curbing the dominance of players congregating near the basket.

The concept is simple.

If a basket is scored from inside the line, you get 2 points. From outside, 3 points.

Initially, the 3–point rule vexed traditionalists, leading to only a handful of attempts per game – perhaps two or three.

To some extent, it demanded courage and a touch of ego to attempt a 3–pointer. Nonetheless, this rule shed light on the fact that proficiency in long-range shooting no longer solely relied on towering height. Stephen Curry, standing at a mere 6' 3", boasts one of the highest completion rates in NBA history.[8] Completion rate assumes significance as data analysis unveiled a notable trend: close to the basket, completion rates were high, but at around 10 feet, they plummeted by half.

---

8   www.bbc.co.uk/sport/extra/zxack0e542/How–Curry–rebuilt–basketball

Consider the intriguing scenario unfolding at the revered 3-point line, situated at approximately 20–23 feet from the basketball basket (with slight variations across diverse leagues). Astonishingly, the rate of successful completions remains remarkably steadfast in this area. Your accuracy at 19 feet is similar to your accuracy at 23 feet.

Now we find ourselves immersed in a captivating predicament, where a marginal 5% decline in accuracy is offset by the astounding potential of a 50% increase in points. Should you happen to watch any basketball games, a ubiquitous sight awaits your discerning eye: players strategically take that crucial step backward, thereby augmenting their overall points tally.

Today, more than 20% of shots fall into the category of '3PAs' – 3 Point Attempts.

As astute marketers, we have much to glean from the fascinating evolution of basketball.

The decision to establish the initial height of the basketball hoop at a towering 10 feet had profound long-term implications on the stature of players. However, as rules underwent transformations, so did the behaviours and physical attributes of these players. Curiously enough, this has resulted in both intended and unintended consequences.

The original set of 13 rules was deliberately crafted, primarily aiming to curtail the tumultuous on-court brawls. Job done. Since then, the sport has accumulated thousands of rules. However, one particular rule, the more recent introduction of the illustrious 3-point line, had an unforeseen impact on the stature of players.

When we embark on the endeavour of designing customer programmes, be it CRM, Loyalty, Recognition or Subscription initiatives, we ought to bear three essential considerations in mind:

Think about the intended consequences of our programmes.

Maintain an open and receptive mindset towards the unintended consequences that may arise.

View our programmes through the lens of evolution, recognising that they may require adaptation and growth over time.

By embracing these thoughtful principles, we can glean valuable insights from the world of basketball and apply them judiciously to our own marketing strategies.

Intended

Even in today's fast-paced marketing landscape, there remains a dearth of thoughtful consideration regarding the true objectives behind CRM, Loyalty, Recognition or Subscription programmes. Instead, we often find ourselves enticed by the allure of technology, eagerly pursuing novel forms of engagement and innovative means of message delivery. This, my friends, leads us into what I affectionately refer to as the treacherous realm of the 'cruel optimism of technology'.

Let me introduce you to the ingenious concept of 'cruel optimism', an idea crafted by the esteemed cultural theorist, Lauren Berlant. Picture this: individuals or groups, driven by their aspirations and desires, become entangled in a complex web. They invest passionately in an object of desire or an ideal that, unbeknownst to them, proves detrimental to their own well-being. It's a paradoxical attachment, offering hope, satisfaction and fulfilment, yet simultaneously obstructing or undermining the very outcomes they seek to achieve.

Cruel optimism exists when something you desire is actually an obstacle to you being able to flourish.

The crux of 'cruel optimism' lies in the heart-wrenching revelation that the very source of hope and optimism one clings to perpetuates its challenges, frustrations or unfulfilled aspirations. It's akin to a relentless trap, ensnaring individuals in an endless cycle of striving. They remain unable to disentangle themselves from what they believe will bring them happiness or stability, oblivious to mounting evidence that exposes its elusive nature or harm.

Oh, how frequently have we been captivated by the seductive allure of a shiny new technological marvel, only to realise that we are inadvertently serving the technology itself rather than catering to the needs of our valued customers? I have spent as many hours convincing organisations that they don't necessarily require the latest and greatest gadgets, just as fervently as I have advocated for the adoption of those tools when truly necessary.

I'm going to suggest five potential high-level approaches which, in combination, will allow you to start thinking about how to plan your engagements – without thinking about technology.

Customer Segmentation and Profiling

Understanding who your customers are is the cornerstone of all marketing efforts. This involves collecting and analysing data to identify distinct groups within your customer base. This can include age, gender, purchasing habits, online behaviour, and so forth. A simple framework for this approach could be a step-by-step plan on data collection, analysis and the development of customer personas.

Personalised Marketing and Communication

Once you have segmented your customers into groups, you can create personalised marketing campaigns that speak directly to each. This might involve personalised emails, product recommendations, targeted offers and content tailored to their preferences and behaviour. The framework here would involve a content strategy, personalisation techniques and the subsequent marketing automation tools that allow for personalisation at scale. More on personalisation in a later perspective.

Customer Journey Mapping and Touchpoint Optimization

The customer journey map is a visual representation of the customer's experience with your brand. It helps identify the various stages the customer goes through and highlights opportunities to engage with him/her effectively. It's important to optimise each touchpoint for maximum impact. Your framework here could outline the stages of the customer journey, key touchpoints and strategies for improvement at each stage. More on this one in the 'Pass Go and Collect £200' perspective.

Loyalty and Retention Programmes

Building customer loyalty is crucial for repeat business and brand advocacy. This can involve loyalty programmes, rewards for referrals, exclusive offers for repeat customers and enhanced customer service. Your framework here would be a detailed plan on how to implement and manage such programmes, how to communicate them to the customers, and how to measure their success.

Feedback and Continuous Improvement

Listening to your customers is key to improving their experience and your offerings. This can be done through customer surveys, social media listening and data analysis. Implementing changes based on this feedback can lead to continuous improvement and increased customer satisfaction. The framework for this approach should detail the feedback collection methods, analysis and steps for implementing changes based on the insights gained.

Each of these approaches should be presented with clear objectives, strategies, tactics and performance measures. It's important to align them with the overall business strategy and to ensure they are customer-focused and data-driven. Remember that each brand is unique, so these frameworks should be adaptable to the specific context in which you're operating.

Allow me to share some thinking from my tenure as the Global Head of CRM at Aesop. During this remarkable journey, I had the privilege of assisting the organisation in crafting their CRM and Loyalty Strategies. To achieve this, I devised a simple, yet powerful framework known as the 'Axes of Recognition', an approach that guided the development of each programme, ensuring it resonated deeply with customers and left a lasting impact.

Not complicated but then, as I have alluded to previously, I'm no rocket scientist.

This thinking could be applied both at a high level (using it to define the key behaviours a loyalty programme should focus on) to very tactical (what exactly is this email meant to do?).

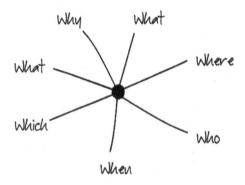

Axes of Recognition

Here are some starting thoughts around which marketing programmes can be built.

1. Who

– Who can we turn into brand advocates to influence other potential customers?

– Who are our highest-value customers that we should focus on retaining?

– Who are potential customers that are not yet engaged with our brand?

– Who among our customers would be most responsive to a referral programme?

– Who is buying our products only during the gifting season?

2. What

– What behaviours can we encourage to increase average order value?

– What needs can we identify and fulfil with new product offerings?

– What can we do to make our customers' journeys more convenient and seamless?

– What types of content can we create that will resonate with our customers?

– What incentives can we provide to increase customer loyalty?

3. When

– When are the best times to target our customers with specific marketing messages?

– When can we prompt customers to re-engage with our brand?

– When should we introduce seasonal products or promotional offers?

– When is it appropriate to ask for reviews or referrals?

– When should we expect a surge in demand so that we can manage inventory better?

4. Where

– Where can we find potential customers who aren't yet aware of our brand?

– Where can we interact with our customers to build a stronger brand community?

– Where can we position our advertisements for maximum visibility?

– Where should we focus our sales efforts: online or physical locations?

– Where are our most profitable customers buying our products?

5. Why

– Why do customers choose us and how can we reinforce these reasons in our messaging?

– Why do customers abandon their shopping carts and how can we minimise this behaviour?

– Why do customers return products and how can we address these issues?

– Why do customers switch to competitors and how can we prevent this?

– Why do some customers refer us to others and how can we encourage more referrals?

6. Which

– Which marketing strategies have been the most successful and how can we replicate them?

– Which customer needs are currently unmet and how can we meet them?

– Which marketing channels are most profitable and how can we optimise them?

– Which customer segments have the highest potential for growth?

– Which customers are loyal to a specific product or product category?

7. How

– How can we enhance customer experience to improve retention?

– How can we utilise customer feedback to improve our products or services?

- How can we personalise our communication to engage each customer segment better?

- How can we motivate customers to engage more with our content?

- How can we maximise the lifetime value of our customers?

Each of these questions focuses on understanding, influencing and creating strategies around customer behaviours to drive marketing outcomes.

How did some of these translate into actionable programmes for Aesop?

Who is Buying our Products only During the Gifting Season?

Aesop is renowned for being a generous brand and we found that we had generous customers, many of whom would only shop with us once a year during the festive season (Christmas or Peak in most retailers' language). The one thing we didn't want to do was stop this display of generosity, but we did want to encourage further purchases. The thinking resulted in us encouraging them to potentially 'gift themselves' but also to highlight the other gifting opportunities in the calendar year.

Which Customers are Loyal to a Specific Product or Product Category?

This manifested itself when our Parsley Seed Anti-Oxidant Intense Serum (PSAOIS) underwent a slight reformulation. As a means of recognition of our dedicated PSAOIS customers, we:

- elicited their feedback on the new formulation prior to launch (this was particularly useful as it helped refine our 'How to use' advice)

- invited these loyal PSAOS customers to the initial instore and online consultation workshops
- gave them early access to the product at launch.

How Can We Motivate Customers to Engage More with our Content?

The intention here was not only to get customers to engage with our content but, more specifically, to also target those new customers who received Aesop Gift Sets during the festive season. Aligned with the brand's cultural credentials, a QR code on each gift set led recipients and buyers alike to a short story that was aligned with that particular array of products. Not only did this increase content engagement across the board but it also helped new customers find content about how to use their products. Products used in the correct manner resulted in better efficacy and therefore happier, repeat customers.

<u>Unintended</u>

2+2=5

An anthropologist is told by a remote tribesman that 2+2=5. The anthropologist asks how this is possible. The tribesman says 'By counting of course. First, I tie two knots in a piece of rope. Then I tie another two knots in another piece. When I tie the two ropes together, I have five knots'

'One thing a person cannot do, no matter how rigorous his analysis or how heroic his imagination, is to draw up a list of things that would never occur to him.'

Thomas Schelling Cold War Strategist

Let's never forget that at the other end of strategy and tactic is a human being and if I might for a moment, I digress back to my days as an astrophysicist.

The Heisenberg Uncertainty Principle

Heisenberg's Uncertainty Principle in quantum mechanics states that it is impossible to precisely measure the exact position and momentum of a particle at the same time. Applying this principle to the world of customers, we can't always precisely predict what a customer will do next (momentum) and know their current state (position) with perfect accuracy. However, personalisation thrives in this uncertainty. By using probabilistic models and continually updating our understanding based on new data, we can navigate this uncertainty and adapt our marketing strategies to align better with each customer's unique journey. But we will never get to being 100% correct because, well, customers are human beings.

Unpredictability in customer behaviour results in our inability to predict with absolute certainty how a customer will respond to a particular product, service or marketing campaign. This inherent characteristic of human nature is influenced by a multitude of factors including personal preferences, changing circumstances, market trends, and more.

Here are some ways you could describe it.

1. Complexity: Customer behaviour is complex and multifaceted. It is influenced by a wide variety of factors – from individual personality traits to social and cultural influences. This complexity makes it challenging to predict with absolute accuracy.

2. Dynamic Nature: Customer preferences and behaviours are constantly changing. This dynamism makes predictability a moving target. Trends evolve, new products and services enter the market and individual life circumstances change – all impacting customer behaviours.

3. Individual Differences: Each customer is unique, with his/her own set of preferences, needs and desires. This individuality makes it hard to predict behaviour based on group trends or averages.

4. Emotional Factors: Decisions are often influenced by emotions, which can be unpredictable and difficult to measure. Customers might make impulse purchases or be swayed by a brand's story or values, factors which are hard to anticipate.

5. External Influences: External factors such as market changes, global events, technological advancements and more, can drastically shift customer behaviours in unpredictable ways.

While unpredictability is a challenge in CRM, personalisation and marketing automation, it also presents an opportunity. By leveraging personalisation techniques, machine learning and AI (Artificial Intelligence), businesses can understand and anticipate customer behaviours better. Even if they can't predict them with 100% accuracy, they can use these tools to improve their understanding significantly and increase the chances of meeting customers' needs and desires.

Stuff Just Happens

Waitrose introduced a free coffee or tea perk for their MyWaitrose loyalty card members in 2014. This move was indeed controversial because some customers complained that the stores were being flooded by people who were only there for the free coffee and not buying anything else. Waitrose responded to this later by changing the rules to require a purchase before a free coffee could be obtained.

In 2012, McDonald's launched a Twitter campaign using the hashtag #McDStories, hoping customers would share positive experiences with the brand. However, the campaign was quickly hijacked by users sharing negative stories and McDonald's had to withdraw the hashtag within two hours.

In Australia, Domino's had a promotion where if you were spotted with a Domino's logo (from a magnet they distributed), you could win free pizza for a year. However, the magnets ended up being stolen off cars and even purchased from eBay by those seeking to win, leading to a lot of complaints.

But can we plan for this?

Donald Rumsfeld made the following statement during a Department of Defense news briefing on February 12, 2002.

'Reports that say that something hasn't happened are always interesting to me, because as we know, there are known knowns; there are things we know we know. We also know there are known unknowns; that is to say we know there are some things we do not know. But there are also unknown unknowns – the ones we don't know we don't know. And if one looks throughout the history of our country and other free countries, it is the latter category that tends to be the difficult ones.'

This quote became quite well-known owing to its philosophical nature and the complex ideas it conveys about the nature of knowledge and uncertainty, particularly in the context of national security. It has since been widely applied in a variety of other fields, including business and marketing.

For example:

1. Known Knowns: These are the things we are certain about and have clear data or evidence to support. For example, it's a well-known fact that social media platforms like

Facebook and Instagram have a significant influence on consumer behaviour. A specific case could be Nike's 'Just Do It' campaign which leverages social media influencers and celebrities to promote their products. This campaign has successfully driven brand engagement and sales.

2. Known Unknowns: These are things we know we don't understand fully or need more information about. For example, in the wake of the Cambridge Analytica scandal, Facebook changed its algorithms, making them more opaque to advertisers. Marketers knew they didn't fully understand how these new algorithms would impact their ad reach and consumer engagement, representing a known unknown.

3. Unknown Knowns: These are things we know but aren't consciously aware of or don't actively put into practice. For instance, with the rise of big data, companies often sit on a wealth of customer information without realising its potential. An example is Tesco's realisation of the value of its Clubcard programme data. Dunnhumby, a customer data science company, helped Tesco analyse these data, leading to personalised promotions that significantly increased sales and customer loyalty.

4. Unknown Unknowns: These are things we don't even know that we don't know, typically representing future events or trends that take us by surprise. An example of this is the COVID-19 pandemic. Brands and marketers couldn't have predicted the pandemic's enormous impact on consumer behaviour, such as the massive shift to online shopping and the boom in home fitness and entertainment products.

Applying the Knowns and Unknowns framework in marketing helps to understand and navigate the uncertainties and certainties in consumer behaviour and market trends.

It encourages proactive learning and adaptability, critical components of successful marketing strategies.

But ultimately it's about being agile enough across People:Process:Tech to be prepared for stuff just happening.

Evolution

The Evolution of the Peppered Moth

This is a classic example of natural selection in action, often cited in biology textbooks. Before the Industrial Revolution in England, the peppered moth predominantly existed in a light colouration, which helped it hide from predators on the bark of trees. However, as pollution from the Industrial Revolution darkened the trees with soot, the once-rare dark variant of the moth became increasingly common because it was now better camouflaged against predators, whereas the light-coloured moths became easy targets.

'Everyone has a plan until they get punched in the mouth.' The words of Mike Tyson the well-known boxer and less-known strategist.

Tyson, a former professional boxer, often used this quote to highlight how even the best strategies can quickly fall apart under pressure or when confronted with an unexpected challenge. It has since been widely quoted in various contexts outside of boxing to emphasise the importance of adaptability and resilience.

It's not quite original. It seems to be referring to a quote attributed to Helmuth von Moltke the Elder, a German field marshal in the nineteenth century. He's famous for the concept: 'No plan survives contact with the enemy.'

This quote essentially means that all strategic plans will inevitably need to change once they are put into action and face real-world opposition. It underscores the importance of flexibility and the ability to adapt quickly to changing circumstances, much like Mike Tyson's quote about everyone having a plan until they get punched in the face. Both quotes convey a similar message about adaptability and the unpredictability of real-world situations.

The only constant is change, as they say, and this will always be reflected in your customer-facing programmes.

Going back to my basketball story. Originally Naismith had but one rule – get the ball into the opposition's basket. Very quickly he established the first 13 rules, mainly to stop the brawling that started to take place during the game. There are now literally hundreds, if not thousands, of rules that play a role in how the game has evolved. In fact, an interesting point to note is that the rules can vary depending on which country or basketball association you are playing in. So customer programmes will vary from brand to brand, but also within brands depending on the market in question.

At an event I presented at in 2023, a simple Google search for loyalty programmes that had changed over the past few years resulted in a whole host of brands which had evolved their programmes: Boots, Marks & Spencer, ASDA, Tesco and McDonalds to name but a few.

No customer-facing programme can remain unchanged over time.

Consumer behaviour and expectations change.

The environment, whether that be economic or competitive, changes.

Organisations change!

The key here is to always be ready for change.

1. Use Data to Inform Decisions: Make use of data analysis to understand what customers like, how they behave and emerging trends. This means gathering and examining information from different sources such as social media and website interactions, and buying patterns. This approach helps predict and respond to changes in what customers want.

2. Invest in Modern Flexible Technology: Embrace cutting-edge technologies like artificial intelligence, machine learning and automated tools. These can help tailor experiences to individual customers, make marketing efforts more effective and improve customer service.

3. Flexible Marketing Strategies: Create marketing plans that can change quickly in response to new information and market shifts. This may involve more short-term planning and the ability to change direction based on up-to-date data and customer feedback.

4. Put Customers at the Forefront: Make the customer experience a top priority in all areas of the business. This involves not just understanding current customer needs but also anticipating future preferences. Gaining insights through direct engagement with customers, such as through social media, surveys and direct conversations, is crucial.

5. Keep Learning and Adapting: Stay up to date with market trends, new technologies and shifts in consumer behaviour. Foster a culture within the organisation that

values ongoing learning and the ability to adapt to new situations.

By adopting these strategies, organisations can navigate the complex and ever-changing landscape of customer needs and preferences better, focusing on being adaptable, customer-oriented and innovative.

It's Not Rocket Science

A member of the prestigious Marriott family found himself travelling for business purposes and, owing to the absence of their renowned hotel chain in the area, he resorted to staying at a competitor's establishment. Upon his arrival and as he made his way to the check-in counter, he introduced himself by name. To his surprise, the receptionist at the desk immediately greeted him with a warm, 'Ah, Mr. Marriott, welcome back.' This unexpected recognition left Mr. Marriott both astonished and curious. He knew that creating a system capable of linking multiple venues to offer such personalized, first-response service was not only technologically challenging but also significantly costly. Eager to understand how such a feat was achieved in a competing hotel, Mr. Marriott questioned the receptionist, who initially hesitated to reveal her methods. However, after some persistent inquiry, she finally conceded and explained her technique.

She elaborated: 'You see, Mr. Marriott, the process begins the moment your car pulls up to our front entrance. George, our observant doorman, greets you and casually inquires if you've visited us before. If your response is a yes, he subtly signals me by tugging his ear as he escorts you to my desk. This discreet gesture is my cue. So, when I hear your name, I immediately know to extend a hearty welcome back to you, giving the impression of a connected, attentive service across our establishments.'

Why I Stopped Eating Pizza
for Six Months

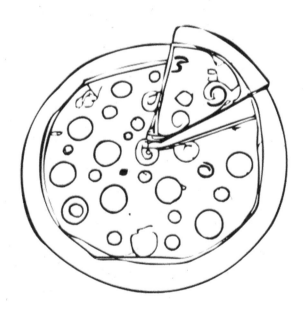

My name – Gianfranco Cuzziol – is a nod to my Italian heritage, but a heritage that might not initially ring true to many ears. I don't boast the typical Italian accent, nor do I embody the quintessential Italian appearance. Yet, I am no less a proud Italian. I am the product of a love story, a unique blend of my father's Venetian steadfastness and my mother's Neapolitan vivacity.

My father, a man as resilient and deep as the canals of Venice, and my mother, embodying all the vibrancy and energy of Naples, instilled in me a spirit that's as rich and contrasting as the Italian landscape. I am a hybrid, a living testimony of the beautiful fusion of these two distinctive cultures.

My Italian essence may not be immediately discernible, but I live it every day in my own ways. My first drink of the day is an espresso. I ride a Vespa, the wind whistling past me reminding me of Italy's timeless style. I cruise the streets in my Fiat 500, a little piece of Italian city efficiency. These seemingly mundane tasks resonate with my roots, subtle affirmations of my cultural lineage.

I know the Italian national anthem by heart, a rhythmic verse that reaffirms my connection to my homeland and I listen to it proudly, or sing along whenever it is played. And then there's pizza. When I make my own pizza, each meticulous layer, each generous sprinkle of cheese, becomes a tribute to Italian craftsmanship and perfection. My hands move, not just with the memory of the process, but with the spirit of my heritage. Pizza is important to me but I never veer from the simple Margherita which, if you don't know, was named to honour Italy's unification, with the three toppings, basil, mozzarella and tomato, representing the green, white and red of the Italian flag. The dish was named after the Queen of Italy, Margherita of Savoy.[9]

While my name is my badge of honour, my daily rituals are my testament to the world of my proud Italian lineage. These actions might not scream Italian, yet they carry within them the essence of my culture, the love for my roots.

In this modern world, I am a convergence of tradition and progression. I might not fit the cliched Italian image, but my story proves that our heritage is far more nuanced. It's not just about appearances or accents. It's about how we live our lives, how we honour our roots and how we manifest our identity amidst a world riddled with stereotypes.

Through my Vespa rides, my Fiat 500 drives, my knowledge of the anthem, my pizza making – I am manifesting what it means to be Italian to me. It's not just about looking or sounding a part; it's about proudly carrying forward and reshaping my heritage. It's the tale of who I am, where I come from, and how I choose to define myself. I take it seriously. Since 2000, in response to France beating Italy in the European Championship final, I have refused to buy French wine. Don't get me started on Brazil nuts!

My journey is a testament to this profound pride. Not just for my Italian heritage, but also for the unique individuality that I bring to it. It's a reminder that our identities have the capacity to be redefined and reinterpreted, while still remaining fundamentally connected to our roots. This is the essence of Gianfranco Cuzziol. Taking the title of one of the songs from the film *The Greatest Showman*: 'This is me!'.

---

9   https://www.atlasobscura.com/places/birthplace-of-the-pizza-margherita

DNA Test

With this in mind I was truly excited when my wife bought me a DNA kit for my birthday. In exchange for a sample of my saliva I was about to 'Discover my heritage, learn about my ancestors and find new family connections'.

Would I be more Venetian than Neapolitan? More Leonardo da Vinci (born in Vinci, Tuscany in 1452, he was an artist and scientist who is widely considered one of the most diversely talented individuals ever to have lived) than Raffaele Esposito (born in Naples, Campania in 1857, a chef often credited with creating the Margherita pizza).

I would even settle for 50/50.

Saliva despatched, I eagerly and impatiently waited for the 6–8 weeks the test would take to get my results back to me.

As the screen blinked one Monday evening, I received an email – my long-anticipated DNA results had arrived. I held my breath, my fingers trembling with a mix of nervousness and excitement. With a glass of my beloved Chianti at my side, I entered the world of my ancestry.

In a twist that could rival an Italian opera's climax, it turned out I wasn't Italian! Not even a smidgen; well, perhaps an eighth at most. Smaller than my regular slice of pizza! Shocked? So was I. I was so taken aback that I couldn't look at a slice of pizza for a whole week! The week became a month. One month became six!

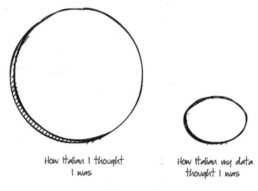

How Italian I thought
I was

How Italian my data
thought I was

Pizza Size

The ink of my story was actually written in the languages of Eastern Europe, dusted with Middle Eastern nuances. My ancestral breakdown was an enigma, a melting pot of cultural identities I had never considered. I was broken down as:

– Europe East: 59%

– Europe South: 14%

– Middle East: 13%

– Europe West: 6%

– Finland/North-west Russia: 4%

– Caucasus: 3%

– Iberian Peninsula: less than 1%

Goulash and Falafel became staples in my fridge!

I shunned the DNA results for a few months, too overwhelmed to dive deeper. That is until, of course, an email, more enticing than the last, found its way to me. Its subject line? ' Your updated DNA results'. With a renewed spirit (and a glass of Bulgarian red for comfort), I returned to the world of my heritage, eyes wide and expectations held at bay.

Joy, surprise and a touch of triumph washed over me as I scanned my revised results:

- Eastern Europe and Russia: 36% (with traces from the Czech Republic, Slovakia, Poland, and Lithuania)
- Italy: 32% (primarily from the southern regions of Lazio and Campania)
- Baltic States: 29%
- Greece and the Balkans: 3%

I was Italian, after all! Well, one-third at least. To celebrate, I treated myself to a pizza feast, trading the Bulgarian red for Chianti once again. I think I may have even dabbled with a slice of tiramisu![10]

Yet, questions remained. Why this discrepancy? My DNA couldn't possibly have changed. It was, after all, the most fundamental part of me – of anybody! In search of answers, I found an enlightening article that lent me some comfort. And thus, my journey into understanding my past, and data, continued.

1 – Reflections on References

Let's take a stroll down the bustling DNA avenue, where Ancestry DNA is but one among a myriad of establishments offering to delve into your genetic mysteries. Your 'ethnicity' essentially comes to life by comparing your DNA with a curated catalogue of their reference samples.

Picture my surprise that when I first dipped my toes into this world, it seems that only a modest library of 3,000 reference

---

10 As I write in January 2024, I am now 44% Southern Italian. Maybe I will go for the Alfa Romeo Giulia next.

samples was available. Lo and behold, by the time of my DNA update, this collection had mushroomed to a whopping 16,000 samples! Now, in the futuristic year of 2024, Ancestry DNA boasts an impressive 71,000 DNA samples in their reference repertoire.

So, if the original data set was biased in some way (purely as result of what DNA had been collected up until that point) then that would have steered my results in a particular direction. For all those CRM data analysts that I've tried to ignore when running my hypotheses on direct mail and email campaigns, here's what you have been waiting for. I apologise for having dismissed you as party poopers.

While a larger reference pool theoretically enhances accuracy, there's still a catch: potential geographical bias. Think of it as their treasure trove being more inclined to samples from regions where their collection campaigns were more successful. This skew reminds me of the infamous polling error during the 1936 U.S. presidential election.

The Literary Digest, predicting an Alf Landon triumph over President Roosevelt, committed a classic sampling error. They polled people from their magazine readership, car owners and telephone users – a selection that leaned heavily towards the wealthy and, consequently, the Republicans. Yet, a 1937 poll by George Gallup found that wealthier respondents actually favoured Roosevelt. The bias arose from the reluctance of Roosevelt supporters to partake in the *Digest's* poll.

2 – Defining Definitions

Have you ever grappled with the tricky concept of bias in AI algorithms? If not, here's a bite-sized primer. Automated decision making hinges on initial models and existing data, both of which can inadvertently carry bias from previous work and experiences. The consequences? Potential discrimination on racial and gender grounds, for example.

– In 2019, a study discovered a healthcare algorithm used by hospitals across the US to allocate extra care favoured white patients over sicker black patients. The algorithm relied on health costs as a proxy for health needs, and because of systemic inequalities leading to less spending on healthcare for black patients, they were systematically disadvantaged.[11]

– AI recruiting tools could inadvertently shape the candidate pool and narrow the funnel by placing priority on getting candidate clicks and not on attracting the best candidate.[12]

DNA companies each interpret geographic regions according to their unique metrics. Some amalgamate countries into larger regions; others may focus on parts of a single country. It's essentially an interpretive dance with data choreographed to set them apart in the bustling DNA marketplace.

Post Hoc Hergo Propter Hoc

Every morning my grandmother would step out of her house in Italy and shout 'Let this house be safe of tigers!' Then she goes on with the rest of her day.

After a couple of weeks of seeing this, I ask her, 'What are you doing? There isn't a tiger within a thousand kilometres of here.'

He said, 'See? It works!'

In the pantheon of intellectual giants and creative masterminds, the story of Abraham Wald shines as an example of how data

---

11 https://www.nature.com/articles/d41586-019-03228-6
12 https://hbr.org/2019/05/all-the-ways-hiring-algorithms-can-introduce-bias

can, and should, be viewed from many angles to innovate better.

Born in the modest town of Cluj within the former Austro-Hungarian Empire, Wald's life and seminal theories consistently defied convention, charting less-trodden paths and shattering prevailing paradigms.

Abraham Wald

The foundations of Wald's intellectual journey were laid in the esteemed University of Vienna. Guided by the eminent mathematician Hans Hahn, Wald delved deep into the abstract world of pure mathematics. However, upon obtaining his Ph.D. in 1931, he encountered an unexpected hurdle. His Jewish heritage proved to be an impediment in procuring a university position amidst a brewing anti-Semitic climate.

Consequently, Wald found himself at the Austrian Institute for Business Cycle Research, transitioning from pure mathematics to statistical analysis – an unanticipated shift that would later decisively influence the course of World War II.

As the 1930s ebbed away, Europe was caught in the throes of escalating anti-Semitic persecution. Wald, like many of his contemporaries, was compelled to abandon his homeland in search of safety. His destination was America, a move that signified more than just a geographical transition – it marked the metamorphosis of a scholarly mathematician into a crucial wartime strategist.

In the United States, Wald found himself amidst an innovative initiative taking root at Columbia University – the Statistical Research Group (SRG). As the war clouds loomed ominously, the American government acknowledged the latent potential of statistical analysis for confronting military challenges. An assembly of statisticians was gathered, Wald among them, and bankrolled to devise mathematical solutions to pressing wartime problems.

World War II was raging, with the United States suffering substantial losses of bomber aircraft. The implications were manifold: economic, strategic and psychological. An urgent challenge surfaced – to protect the aircraft while retaining their operational efficacy. It was here that Wald's statistical acumen intersected with the exigencies of war.

The military grappled with a quandary: where to place armour on their bomber planes? Armour offered safety, yet it also introduced weight, hindering operational efficiency. Initial inspections of returning planes revealed a pattern of damage, with more bullet holes in specific areas. The ostensible solution was to place more armour where the damage was most prevalent.[13]

---

13 For the record, in the same way that you can't build a plane with the same material used for the black boxes they carry, you couldn't make the whole of a military bomber of heavy protective material.

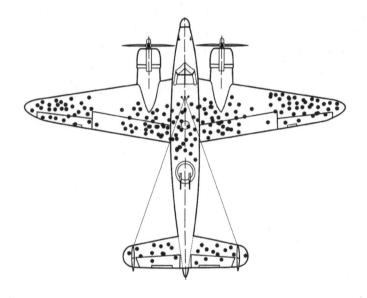

However, Abraham Wald, the unconventional thinker, perceived things differently. He examined the same data but from a unique perspective, an ability that set him apart. His suggested solution was to put the armour not where everyone was looking, but where they weren't. Contradicting prevalent military wisdom, Wald proposed armouring the undamaged parts of the planes, surmising that hits in these areas were fatal, thus preventing those planes from returning. He introduced the concept of survivorship bias, redirecting the Allies' strategic approach in an unexpected yet highly effective direction.

Wald's impact wasn't confined to aircraft armour. He also applied his novel thinking in the domain of munition testing. Wald's sequential analysis was pivotal when resources were limited and efficiency was critical. His innovative approach to quality testing – examining ammunition piece-by-piece rather than in entire batches, marked a significant departure from established norms, saving valuable resources and time.

The reverberations of Wald's established principles continue to influence various spheres of human endeavours. His pioneering work in decision making under uncertainty made significant contributions to operations research, a nascent field during the war. Wald's statistical decision theory continues to guide decisions taken amid uncertain circumstances and it has permeated diverse fields, ranging from economics to computer science.

Understanding your frame of reference and having clear definitions has always played an important role in the world of CRM to help understand the data you have to improve your marketing efficiency and effectiveness.

Marketing Efficiency: This refers to the optimization of resources within your marketing efforts. Think of it as the 'how' in your strategy. Efficiency is about minimising costs, time and effort while still achieving the intended output. This would be akin to optimising your operational levers – reducing waste, automating processes and leveraging data analytics to refine targeting. It's about getting the most out of every dollar spent, every hour invested and every campaign executed.

Marketing Effectiveness: This is the 'what' and 'why' of your marketing strategy. It's about the impact and results of your marketing activities. Effectiveness is measured by how well your marketing efforts meet your strategic objectives, such as increasing brand awareness, market share or return on investment.

While marketing efficiency is about doing things right, marketing effectiveness is about doing the right things. Efficiency focuses on the optimization of resources, whereas effectiveness is concerned with the strategic impact and outcomes of your marketing activities. Both are crucial, but they serve different roles in the grand scheme of a successful marketing strategy.

One of the key models I have used is the Recency, Frequency, Value (RFV) model.[14] An RFV model is a simplistic marketing analysis tool used to identify and rank customers based on three quantitative factors:

1. Recency (R): When was the last time the customer made a purchase? This element considers the time elapsed since the customer's most recent transaction, with the assumption that customers who have bought from you recently are more likely to buy again compared with those who haven't interacted with your business for a while.

2. Frequency (F): How often does the customer purchase from the business? This assesses the number of transactions a customer has made over a specified period. Frequent buyers are considered more likely to continue to do business with you.

3. Value (V): How much does the customer spend? This can be calculated as the average spend per purchase or the total spend over a certain period. Customers who spend more are considered more valuable to the business.

These three dimensions of customer behaviour are used to score and segment customers, usually on a scale of 1 to 5 for each parameter. The higher the score, the more valuable the customer is likely to be to the business. The RFV model

---

14 Note I am using RFV rather than RFM where M describes monetary value. I use value in my description to talk about revenue, but value also comes in many other forms, for example advocacy.

provides a simple, quantifiable way for businesses to identify their most valuable customers and to target their marketing efforts more effectively.

In essence, the RFV model can be used to predict future customer behaviour based on past interactions. It provides an insight into which customers are most likely to respond to promotional efforts and make purchases, helping businesses allocate their marketing resources more efficiently.

But there are certainly pros and four cons of Recency, Frequency, Value models:

Pros

1. Customer Segmentation: RFV models provide a simple and effective way of segmenting customers based on purchasing behaviour. This can help businesses target marketing communications and offers to different groups of customers better.

2. Predictive Power: By examining past purchasing behaviour, RFV models can help businesses predict which customers are most likely to make purchases in the future. This can assist in the efficient allocation of marketing resources.

3. Profitability Analysis: The (Monetary) Value component of the RFV model allows businesses to identify their most profitable customers. This can guide strategic decisions about customer relationship management and retention efforts.

Cons

1. Too Simplistic: While the simplicity of RFV models is generally an advantage, it can also be a limitation. By focusing only on recency, frequency, and monetary value, RFV models overlook other potentially significant

factors, such as customer satisfaction, product preferences or demographic information.

2. Short-term Focus: RFV models are based on recent behaviour and may not fully capture long-term customer value. For example, a customer who makes large, infrequent purchases might be undervalued in an RFV analysis.

3. Assumption of Independence: RFV models assume that recency, frequency, and value are independent variables, but in reality, they may be interrelated. For example, a customer who purchases frequently is also likely to have purchased recently.

4. Need for Regular Updating: Customer behaviour can change over time because of a variety of factors. Therefore, RFV models need to be updated regularly with fresh data to maintain their accuracy and usefulness. This can add to the complexity and cost of maintaining these models.

I've often started my engagements at organisations with an RFV analysis. It not only brings to life some of the customer numbers, but also acts as a benchmark for how easy it is to access and interrogate the data you have.

A second and perhaps more useful model can be built around the building of cohorts. Cohort analysis is a type of behavioural analytics that groups users based on shared characteristics and examines their behaviour over time. This analytical model enables businesses to gain insights into the life cycle patterns of customers and observe how these patterns affect the performance of the business.

A 'cohort' refers to a group of users who share a common characteristic within a defined period. This characteristic could be the date of their first purchase, the acquisition channel through which they came to make that purchase, the type of product they first purchased, or any other definable characteristic.

For example, a cohort could be all customers who signed up for a subscription service in January 2023. Over time, businesses can track this cohort to understand its engagement patterns, retention rates and other metrics.

Cohort analysis helps answer questions such as:

– How does the behaviour of customers acquired through different channels change over time?

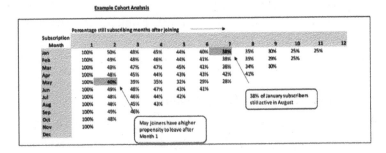

Example Cohort Analysis

– Do customers who make large initial purchases have a higher life-time value?

– Are we getting better at retaining customers over time?

– Does a change in product or marketing strategy positively affect customer retention or purchasing behaviour?

By identifying patterns and trends within different cohorts, businesses can make more informed decisions to optimise their strategies and improve customer retention and monetization. They can be an invaluable tool for understanding how changes in a product or strategy affect different groups of users over time.

Within the dynamic world of retail, understanding the nuances of customer behaviour is paramount. The following are practical examples to illustrate the application of both segment-driven and temporal-engagement cohorts.

Segment-driven Personalisation Cohorts in Retail

1. Device Preference Cohort

– Example: Customers who predominantly shop using mobile devices might have different browsing and purchasing habits compared with those using desktop computers.

– Action: Tailor the shopping experience by optimising mobile ads and ensuring the mobile interface of the online store is user-friendly and intuitive. Implement marketing automation to send targeted offers or reminders to mobile users.

2. Product Category Affinity Cohort

– Example: Customers who frequently purchase skincare products may have different needs and preferences from those buying fashion accessories.

– Action: Use CRM to identify and group these customers. Then create personalised newsletters with expert skincare tips or exclusive discounts on new skincare products.

3. Geographic Location Cohort

– Example: Customers from urban areas might have different purchasing patterns compared with those from suburban or rural locales.

– Action: Personalise marketing campaigns with location-specific offers or product suggestions. For instance, a winter coat promotion might be more relevant for customers in colder regions.

Temporal Engagement Cohorts in Retail

1. First-time Purchase Cohort

– Example: Customers who made their first purchase during a seasonal sale event, such as a 'Summer Sale'.

– Action: Engage them with post-purchase follow-ups, recommending complementary items. Use marketing automation to schedule a series of emails, thanking them and introducing them to loyalty programmes or upcoming events.

2. Loyalty Programme Anniversary Cohort

– Example: Customers who joined the loyalty programme a year ago.

– Action: Celebrate their 'anniversary' by sending personalised offers or bonus points. This can enhance retention and encourage them to continue engaging with the brand.

3. Abandoned Cart Cohort

– Example: Customers who added items to their cart during the Christmas period but didn't complete the purchase.

– Action: Use CRM data to trigger personalised reminder emails or targeted advertisements showcasing the items left in the cart, perhaps with a limited-time discount or free shipping incentive.

These cohorts offer invaluable insights into the diverse and ever-evolving landscape of retail customer behaviour. By leveraging the data, retailers can craft bespoke experiences that not only resonate but also drive loyalty and growth.

A company manager is flying across the desert in a hot air balloon when he realises he is lost. He calls down to a man riding a camel below him and asks where he is.

The man replies, 'You're 42 degrees and 12 minutes, 21.2 seconds north, 122 degrees, 10 minutes west, 212 metres above sea level, heading due east-by-north-east.'

'Thanks,' replies the balloonist. 'By the way, are you a data analyst?'

'Yes,' replies the man. 'How did you know?'

'Everything you told me was totally accurate, you gave me way more information than I needed and I still have no idea what I need to do.'

'I'm sorry,' replied the camel-riding analyst. 'By the way, are you a company manager?'

'Yes,' said the balloonist. 'How did you know?'

'Well,' replied the analyst, 'you've got no idea where you are, no idea what direction you're heading in, you got yourself into this fix by blowing a load of hot air, and now you expect me to get you out of it.'

One of the biggest gripes my analytics team had was being brought in half way through a project to 'do some analysis'.

They were essentially coming in, not knowing anything about the project, its objectives or where the data was coming from, but being asked to prove to the client that it was working! Thanks for that, account management.

This pointless exercise was overcome by insisting that any project began with some form of Measurement and Evaluation exercise. Bigger projects were given a workshop to look at this, while for smaller projects it was undertaken via Slack or Google Docs. But essentially it covered these key areas.

Objective Setting and Prioritisation – where do you want to be and why?

In theory, the project comes with this already agreed. In reality, Marketing and Sales have different views, Head Office wants something different from the Country Manager and they are all on a different planet from the local team. The bigger the client the bigger the differences. It's often only by getting as many of the stakeholders into the room as possible that common ground can be found. I've literally sat in one of these sessions for a large automotive brand where the local teams have demanded a project be delayed because the 'trial's objectives' didn't match their sales objectives.

It is fundamentally asking the question – what needs to happen for this to be deemed a success?

Making Objectives Smarter

Down to the nitty gritty. We need to answer these fundamental questions.

What metrics are we going to associate with the objective?

Is there a benchmark to be achieved? In fact, what is the range within which we need to operate? If we go below a certain threshold, is that the trigger for action? (Remember we are talking about actionable metrics.)

What's the time frame over which the measurement is to be taken?

And remember that frequency is important. Measuring alone often is not the answer. The frequency needs to be a reflection of the environment in which you are operating.

Learning Indicators

Previously, we've talked about using averages. Here is where we decide how we can essentially eliminate the need to use an overall average and drill into useful learning opportunities about how well a project/marketing campaign/process is working by product, segment and region.

Data Source Mapping

This essentially asks where the data is coming from, how frequently and who is responsible for its delivery. The bigger the project the more disparate the sources. A project we ran for a sports brand looking at understanding consumers at retail level included data from:

1 – the store EPOS and colleague interviews
2 – digital activations in the store monitoring footfall, emotions and engagement
3 – mystery shopping and exit interviews
4 – digital conversations.

And each of these streams came from different internal departments or external agencies, each with different priorities, objectives, definitions, data sources and standards.

What should you be measuring?

One key tip is not to measure too much; it just ends up being a distraction from the day job but *the* most basic element of the measurement plan is understanding exactly what you are going to measure.

Five metric types stand out.

Inputs – simply measuring the resources being put into the organisation's efforts at whatever they are growing, reducing, improving. Useful investment metrics for inputs are spending by, for example, objective, geography, medium, customer segment and marketing programme.

Outputs – track the immediate impact of any activities by measuring the customer engagement of the campaign (views, shares, opens, clicks etc)

Outcomes – measure whether you are achieving your goals, i.e., whether marketing objectives are being achieved through measures such as: market share, brand awareness, NPS (Net Promoter Score).

Milestones – progress against a declared goal, e.g., decrease in churn rate of 5% by the end of the first quarter.

Ratios – often finance biased and a combination of the above, e.g., Return on Investment (ROI). They can often be the single metric based on an amalgamation of several others, e.g., Social Momentum or Emotion Index.

External Benchmarks are Pointless

A young married couple moves into a new apartment and decides to repaper the dining room. They call on a neighbour who has a dining room the same size and ask, 'How many rolls of wallpaper did you buy when you papered your dining room?' 'Seven,' he said. So the couple buy seven rolls of expensive paper and then start papering. When they get to the end of the fourth roll, the dining room is finished. Annoyed, they go back to the neighbour and say, 'We followed your advice, but we ended up with three extra rolls!'

'So,' he says, 'that happened to you too!'

Il Canto degli Italiani

The Italian national anthem is actually six verses long but at most sporting occasions you will hear verse one sung twice followed by the chorus twice, with a thumping 'Si!' at the end of the second chorus.

Fratelli d'Italia,
l'Italia s'è desta,
dell'elmo di Scipio
s'è cinta la testa.
Dov'è la Vittoria?
Le porga la chioma,
ché schiava di Roma
Iddio la creò.
Coro
Stringiamci a coorte,
siam pronti alla morte.
Siam pronti alla morte,
l'Italia chiamò.
Stringiamci a coorte,
siam pronti alla morte.
Siam pronti alla morte,
l'Italia chiamò!

Si!

OR …

Brothers of Italy

Italy has risen,

bound Scipio's helmet

Upon her head.

Where is Victory?

Let her bow down

Because as a slave of Rome

God did create her.

Chorus

Let us join in a cohort

we are ready for death

We are ready for death,

Italy has called!

Yes!

Pass Go and Collect £200

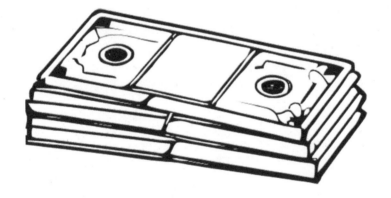

Across civilizations and through the corridors of time, board games have etched their mark on the cultural psyche of societies. From the banks of the Nile to the digital lounges of the twenty-first century, these tactile pursuits have proved to be more than mere diversions. But what gives them their enduring allure?

You could argue that at their core, board games are a reflection of the human need for competition, collaboration and storytelling. They serve as mirrors to the zeitgeist of their times, capturing economic trends, societal norms, and cultural shifts. They engage our cognitive faculties, challenging us to strategise, to negotiate and to deduce. Yet, they also tap into our intrinsic desire for social interaction, drawing players together in shared narratives, be it around ancient Egyptian boards, modern tabletops or a digital screen.

Playing board games has often been seen as a sign of intelligence and evidence of leadership skills. The list of nine skills that a Norse nobleman had to master included the ability to play board games.

Moreover, board games, in their myriad forms, have always provided a safe space for individuals to confront larger themes – war, economics, exploration and diplomacy – allowing players to grapple with these concepts in a controlled environment. They allow us to don the hats of emperors, traders, warriors and detectives, providing a window into worlds both familiar and fantastical. You can even be a landlord.

When we delve into some of the most iconic board games through the ages, we're not just exploring games; we're embarking on a journey through time, understanding the ethos of civilizations and tracing the evolution of social interaction. From the spiritual corridors of ancient Egypt with Senet to the digital integration of the modern game Chronicles of Crime, let's embark on this game-filled voyage and uncover the stories they tell and why they continue to captivate the human spirit.

1. Senet (c. 3500 BC)

Senet is one of humanity's oldest recorded board games. Originating from the cradle of civilization, Ancient Egypt, depictions of this game have been found in burial sites, including the tomb of the famed Tutankhamun. The game board consists of a grid of 30 squares, often beautifully adorned. The exact rules remain somewhat of a mystery, but it's believed to involve a form of back-and-forth movement with pieces, reflecting the journey of life and the transition to the afterlife. Over the millennia, Senet evolved, but its presence in tombs suggests a profound spiritual significance. It wasn't just entertainment; it bore deep cultural and religious connotations, making it much more than a mere game.

2. Royal Game of Ur (c. 2500 BC)

The Royal Game of Ur, often just called The Game of Ur, transports us back to ancient Mesopotamia. This game, discovered in the Royal Tombs of Ur in present-day Iraq, reveals a richly decorated board that hints at its elite status. Played on a 20-square board, players used tetrahedral dice to dictate movement. The mix of luck (from dice rolls) and strategy (in the movement of the pieces) might have been a reflection of the unpredictability of life and fate. It paints a picture of how the ancients viewed life, luck and destiny, with the game acting as a metaphor. Its rediscovery in the 1920s by Sir Leonard Woolley and its subsequent popularisation provided a unique look into the recreational activities of the ancient elite.

3. Go (c. 500 BC)

Hailing from China, Go – known as Weiqi in its homeland – represents an unbroken link spanning over two millennia, making it one of the world's oldest continuously played board games. Its premise is straightforward: two players place black and white stones on a 19x19 grid, aiming to claim territory. However, beneath this simplicity lies profound strategic depth. Over time, the game moved to neighbouring Korea (Baduk) and Japan (Go). In both its strategy and its philosophy, Go has been likened to the art of war, with treatises written about its tactical depth. It has deeply influenced East Asian culture and is referenced in proverbs, art and literature. Even today, Go tournaments attract massive audiences and professional players in East Asia, illustrating its enduring charm.

4. Chaturanga (c. sixth century AD)

As the sun began to set on the Gupta Empire in India, Chaturanga emerged as a reflection of the era's warfare. Played on an 8x8 grid, it is the earliest known precursor to chess. Its name translates to 'four divisions', representing infantry, cavalry, elephants and chariots – all key components of ancient Indian armies. Unlike the swift games of today, Chaturanga was a slower, more contemplative affair, mirroring the methodical pace of warfare in an age where strategy was paramount. Its deep strategic elements and mimicry of real-life warfare made it a favourite pastime for Indian royalty. As trade routes expanded, Chaturanga laid the foundation for the modern game of chess, influencing cultures from East Asia to Europe.

5. Chess (c. ninth to tenth century AD)

Chess, a game transcending cultures, is a testament to how the ancient Indian game of Chaturanga, mentioned above, could be transformed by various civilizations, from Persians (Shatranj) to medieval Europeans. As it travelled, the game metamorphosed. By the time it reached Europe, it had been enriched with new rules, enhancing its pace and strategy, and iconic pieces like the queen and bishop had been introduced. The game's deep tactical intricacies stood as a metaphor for mediaeval politics and warfare. It was not just the elite's game. Chess clubs emerged, fostering community interactions. During the Renaissance, chess treatises proliferated, refining strategies. Today, with worldwide tournaments and grandmasters from diverse backgrounds, chess remains a unifying emblem of strategy and intellect.

6. Hnefatafl: The Viking Game of Strategy (eighth century AD)

Hnefatafl, often referred to as the King's Table, is a captivating relic from the Viking Age, its origins steeped in the early Norse cultures of Scandinavia. This strategic board game offers a tantalising glimpse into the minds of the Vikings, showcasing their love for strategy, war tactics and entertainment.

The game is characterised by its asymmetrical set-up, where one player's central king and defenders seek to escape the board, while the other player's larger force aims to capture the king. The board itself, typically a grid of 11x11 or 13x13 squares, symbolises a battlefield, echoing the Vikings' seafaring raids and territorial defences.

Historical records and archaeological finds suggest that Hnefatafl was widely played across Northern Europe from the fourth to the twelfth centuries AD. The game's remnants have been unearthed in various Viking settlements, from Ireland to the far reaches of Russia. Its popularity waned with the rise of chess in the region, a game that became synonymous with mediaeval European strategy.

7. Nine Men's Morris (fourteenth to seventeenth century AD)

With roots possibly stretching back to the Roman Empire, Nine Men's Morris experienced its zenith during Europe's Renaissance. Played on a board etched with a series of intersecting lines, players strategically place and move their pieces, aiming to form 'mills' or lines of three. The game's captivating blend of strategy and simplicity made it a favoured pastime, with boards often carved into building facades, public seats, and even churches throughout Europe. Its presence in literary works, notably Shakespeare's A Midsummer Night's Dream, highlights its cultural imprint. Although not as widely played today, the game offers a snapshot into the leisure activities of a bygone era, where strategy and foresight were both entertainment and life skills.

8. Monopoly (1933)

Monopoly, an emblematic representation of twentieth-century capitalism, traces its origins to The Landlord's Game, a creation of Elizabeth Magie designed to illustrate the perils of land accumulation and the Georgist economic philosophy. However, when commercialised by Charles Darrow and then Parker Brothers in the 1930s, its capitalist overtones became its selling point. Set against the backdrop of the Great Depression, Monopoly's fantasy of property acquisition, trading and wealth accumulation struck a chord. The game's iconic tokens, ranging from the thimble to the top hat, became cultural symbols. Over the decades, with countless editions and worldwide sales, Monopoly remains a cultural mainstay, reflecting both the aspirations and critiques of capitalism.

9. Risk (1960s)

At a time when the world was embroiled in geopolitical tensions, Risk emerged, offering players the chance to engage in global domination from their living rooms. Conceived in 1957 by Albert Lamorisse, this game of strategy and chance became an instant hit in the 1960s. The board, a map of the world, became a battlefield where players employed tactics, diplomacy, and sometimes sheer luck, to achieve global supremacy. In the Cold War era, Risk was not just a game; it was a reflection of global politics, offering players a taste of the intricate dance of diplomacy and warfare on a global scale.

10. XCOM: The Board Game (2000s)

As the digital age surged, XCOM: The Board Game, released in 2015, elegantly married traditional board gaming with digital integration. Based on the acclaimed video game series, players collaborate to defend Earth from alien invaders, using an app to enhance gameplay. This app integration, a departure from traditional board gaming, provides dynamic challenges and real-time decisions, heightening tension and immersion. In its blend of the digital and physical, XCOM offers a glimpse into the evolving nature of board games, showcasing how technology can be seamlessly integrated to enhance, rather than replace, traditional gameplay.

11. Chronicles of Crime (2020s)

Chronicles of Crime, developed by David Cicurel in 2018, offers a modern twist to the classic detective genre. Incorporating QR codes and augmented reality (AR), players scour virtual crime scenes and question virtual witnesses, combining traditional board game elements with immersive technology. This blend of tactile and digital gameplay offers a fresh, modern experience. As players solve mysteries, they're not just playing a game; they're inhabiting a narrative, with technology serving as a bridge to deeper immersion. Chronicles of Crime's success signals a future where board games and technology coalesce, crafting rich, interactive narratives.

When playing many of these games, you have to imagine that, for example, the pawn is a foot soldier, taking orders from the King (even though we know the real power lies with the Queen); that you are a landlord building a property empire or a detective solving a mystery.

Using this moment of imagination, perhaps we can think about board games and how each game inherently follows a journey: from set up to playing, and then to the end game. The progression or mechanics of each of these games could metaphorically relate to a 'Customer Journey' where, in marketing, they refer to the complete sum of experiences that customers go through when interacting with a company and brand. Instead of looking at just a part of a transaction or experience, the customer journey documents the full experience of being a customer.

1. Senet: Players move their pieces across the board, facing obstructions and aids, much like a customer's journey with its ups and downs.

2. Royal Game of Ur: The binary dice introduce an element of unpredictability. Similarly, a customer's interaction with a brand can be filled with unexpected events that shape their overall experience.

3. Go: Strategy and territory control are key. This can mirror how businesses strategize to ensure a customer's journey is smooth, retaining them within their 'territory' or brand ecosystem.

4. Chaturanga: Each piece has a different role and movement, similar to the varied touchpoints a customer might encounter on his/her journey with a brand.

5. Chess: The game's deep strategy can be likened to a company's planning for customer engagement, anticipating customer needs and moves ahead of time.

6. Hnefatafl: The Viking Game of Strategy: Players have distinct goals in the way different customers have distinct needs and wants at different stages of the customer journey.

7. Nine Men's Morris: Setting up mills (lines of three) is a central objective. In marketing, aligning multiple touchpoints seamlessly can ensure a successful customer journey.

8. Monopoly: Property acquisition and trading can be likened to a customer's journey of exploring, acquiring and sometimes switching between different brand offerings.

9. Risk: Expansion and defence strategies in the game mirror how businesses expand their customer base while retaining existing customers.

10. XCOM: The Board Game: The real-time strategy and adaptation required can be likened to businesses having to adapt in real time, based on customer interactions and feedback.

11. Chronicles of Crime: The use of modern technology tools for solving mysteries can relate to how businesses leverage technology to understand and enhance the customer journey better.

The title of this Perspective 'Pass Go and Collect £200', obviously relates to Monopoly. While Monopoly is a classic board game known for its competitive and strategic gameplay, it has also generated some interesting stories and events throughout its history.

1. The Origins of Monopoly: As mentioned above, the game of Monopoly has a fascinating origin. It was originally created by Elizabeth Magie in the early twentieth century as The Landlord's Game. Her intention was to teach players about the consequences of land ownership and concentration of wealth. However, it was Charles Darrow who patented a modified version of the game in the 1930s and then sold it to Parker Brothers, leading to its commercial success. The story of how the game evolved from Magie's original idea to the popular Monopoly we know today is a noteworthy historical tale.

2. Monopoly in Prison: During World War II, the British Secret Service smuggled special Monopoly sets into German POW camps. These sets contained hidden maps, compasses and real money to aid captured Allied soldiers in their escape attempts. The story of how Monopoly was used as a tool for escape and resistance is a testament to the game's enduring popularity and adaptability.

3. Longest Game Ever: In 1982, a group of Monopoly enthusiasts played the longest continuous game of Monopoly on record. The game lasted for 70 days, during which the players took short breaks for sleep and food. This impressive feat demonstrates the endurance and dedication of Monopoly enthusiasts.

4. Monopoly World Championships: Monopoly has hosted multiple world championships since 1973, where the best players from around the world compete for the title. These championships have produced their own memorable stories of intense competition and strategy.

5. For instance, in 2015, a life-sized Monopoly board was set up in Trafalgar Square, London, as part of a fundraising event. Players moved around the giant board with real people serving as tokens, and the game raised money for charity.

My favourite? Not a huge surprise surely?

Pizza Monopoly

Board Game Night

Board game night is where you discover who your real friends are. They're the ones who still like you after you've bankrupted them in Monopoly, annihilated them in Risk, and accused them in Cluedo.

While Monopoly may seem like a simple board game, its history is rich with unique stories and events that showcase its enduring popularity and cultural significance. From its origins as a teaching tool to its use in World War II and its role in international championships, Monopoly has no doubt left its mark on gaming history.

The game can elicit a wide range of emotions and monetary outcomes throughout gameplay. Here are some of the highs and lows, both emotionally and monetarily, that players often experience.

Highs

1. Acquiring Prime Properties: One of the highs in Monopoly is when you are successful in acquiring a valuable property, especially the ones with a high rent like Mayfair (Boardwalk – USA) or Park Lane (Park Place – USA). It's a moment of excitement and anticipation for future profits.

2. Getting Out of Jail: If you're in jail and manage to roll doubles to get out, or use a 'Get Out of Jail Free' card, it can feel like a lucky break and a relief.

3. Bankrupting Opponents: Successfully bankrupting your opponents can be a high point, especially when it's a close game. Watching their properties go up for auction and slowly gaining control of the board is a powerful feeling.

Lows

1. Landing on Expensive Properties: Landing on an opponent's property which has houses or hotels can be a major low point. It often results in paying a substantial amount of rent which can deplete your funds quickly.

2. Frequent Visits to Jail: Spending too much time in jail can be frustrating, as it prevents you from collecting rent and making strategic moves on the board.

3. Bankruptcy: Going bankrupt in Monopoly is the ultimate low. Losing all your properties and being out of the game can be emotionally challenging, especially if you were doing well before your downfall.

Monopoly is a game of highs and lows, and the emotional and monetary rollercoaster it provides is part of what makes it a timeless classic.

Yet, the highs and lows experienced in a game of Monopoly can be likened to the highs and lows of a customer's journey or experience with a brand. Just as in the game, customers go through a range of emotions and financial interactions when engaging with a brand. Here's how these parallels can be drawn.

Highs in a Customer's Journey with a Brand

1. Positive Customer Service: Receiving excellent customer service can be a high point for customers. When their enquiries are addressed promptly, issues are resolved efficiently and they feel valued, it creates a positive emotional connection.

2. Special Offers and Discounts: In a similar way to winning auctions in Monopoly, customers often feel a sense of satisfaction when they receive special offers, discounts or loyalty rewards, as they provide added value to their purchases.

3. Successful Problem Resolution: If a customer encounters an issue with a product or service and the brand effectively resolves it to his/her satisfaction, it can turn a negative experience into a high point.

4. Building Trust: Over time, as customers have positive interactions and experiences with a brand, they build trust. This trust can lead to a sense of loyalty and emotional attachment to the brand.

5. Achieving Goals: When customers achieve their goals or fulfil their needs through a brand's products or services, it can be a high point. For example, purchasing a dream car or finding the perfect outfit can be emotionally rewarding.

Lows in a Customer's Journey with a Brand

1. Poor Customer Service: Experiencing unhelpful, rude or slow customer service can be a low point. It can lead to frustration and a negative perception of the brand.

2. Unexpected Costs or Fees: In a way similar to landing on expensive properties in Monopoly, encountering unexpected costs or fees can be a financial low point in a customer's journey. Hidden charges or unclear pricing can lead to dissatisfaction.

3. Product or Service Failures: When a product or service does not meet expectations or it malfunctions, it can be a significant low point. This can result in disappointment, inconvenience and potential brand disloyalty.

4. Loss of Trust: If a brand betrays customer trust through unethical practices, data breaches or other negative actions, it can create a deep emotional low and damage the brand's reputation.

5. Lack of Progress Toward Goals: Customers may feel frustration and disappointment if they do not make progress toward their goals or if a brand's products or services do not align with their needs.

Just like in Monopoly, a customer's journey with a brand is a dynamic experience filled with emotional highs and lows. Brands that consistently deliver positive experiences and effectively address low points can build strong customer loyalty and trust over time. Conversely, repeated negative experiences can drive customers away from a brand. Therefore, understanding and managing the customer journey is crucial for building and maintaining a positive brand reputation.

I've often used games as a feature of strategy presentations to depict the use of data in particular, in customer journeys. I remember using a Snakes and Ladders board in a pitch to

Barratt Homes, using it as an analogy with a house buyer's journey through the ups (ladders) and downs (snakes) of a purchase. Barratt's role was to ensure that at every touchpoint (that is on every square of the board) data should be collected to understand what was happening with those house purchases so that the next best action could be delivered.

I have used Cluedo, where players use deductive reasoning to identify the suspect, to explain to a brand how customer data are gathered and analysed to identify its 'suspects' – the target customer segments. Much like deciphering the identity of a suspect in Cluedo, marketers sift through data to construct detailed customer profiles. They analyse behaviour, preferences and interactions to understand who their customers are, what they desire and how they engage with the brand. This process is akin to the systematic elimination of suspects in Cluedo until the most likely profile is revealed.

I famously informed BMW that it was trying to interact with prospective car buyers like a game of Whack-a-mole, trying to react to a prospective customer raising his/her head over the parapet when in fact it could be using data to predict when and where (and even why) they were about to show their hand. I believe that pitch ended up being recorded and shown to the board in Munich.

Whack a Mole[15]

Customer Journey Planning

From John F. Kennedy's Inaugural Address... to the regional GM meeting: 'Ask not what your customers can do for you—ask what you can do for your customers.'

From Barack Obama's 2008 Victory Speech...having won the budget for a new marketing cloud: 'Yes, we can personalise. Yes, we can understand each customer's unique journey.'

From Winston Churchill's Their Finest Hour speech...at the presentation of the year end CRM results: 'Never in the field of human commerce was so much owed by so many to such tailored marketing strategies.'

But how do you go about designing or, more importantly, understanding the customer journey? And why is it important?

---

15   Image source https://bakadesuyo.com/2012/10/whac-a-mole-teach-ability-focus/

One angle is to think about why customers are loyal to brands.

The answer to this is many faceted but if we put it into three very broad buckets, it's because:

1– you offer them discounts
2– nothing better has come along
3 – they have an emotional bond with you.

I'm going to suggest that the first two are not real loyalty.

However, the customers who have a bond with you emotionally often have that bond because the brand has taken the time to understand each part of the customer journey and tried to match, and hopefully surpass, customer expectations.

That understanding of the customer journey is something I've undertaken many times so I'm going to share briefly where that starts.

The most commonly used customer journey is often seen when mapping out Customer Experience. This is about creating a realistic view of the journey your customers have with your brand. Now please bear in mind that I'm going to focus ultimately on where this leads to with CRM, personalisation, etc. Hopefully that doesn't surprise you. But when you go about creating yours, bear in mind what the intention is.

Do you just want to understand the journey? (Interesting but ultimately pointless.)

Do you want to use it to form a stress test for any changes to a product or service?

Or, where I've used it most, do you want to create a vision of where you want to be in the future across the whole journey, or how CRM/Personalisation specifically can improve that journey?

By the way – it's OK to think about the return you get by improving the experience – your CFO might not be too interested in the customer journey map itself, but he/she will definitely be interested in the ROI document!

It's also OK to focus just on your corner of the world. Don't try and boil the ocean; boiling enough water for a cup of coffee is a good start.

But also at the outset, I'm going to point out that the value of mapping the end to an experience is the process of actually getting people from across the business together and taking a look at what you do from the customer's perspective. It's a really powerful way of getting a group of people inside the business to lift themselves out of their functional roles and look at what they do from a customer's perspective.

The journey below is an early version of a map I helped produce while at Aesop.

Stage	Visit	Trial	Purchase	Early Use	Regular Use	Replenish
Mindset	Absorb	Experiment & Evaluate	Decide	Enthuse	Creature of Habit	Re-evaluate
Our Role	Inspire	Entice	Reassure	Romance	Encourage	Revitalise
Do						
Key Insights		Visual depiction of the customer flow				
Drivers		What does our research tell us?				
Think & Feel		What's driving the customer during this stage?				
Opportunities		What are they thinking about the experience?				
Barriers		What is our opportunity in CRM?				
		What is stopping us ? Data ? Technology? Training?				

Aesop Customer Journey

This is a map which we're building over time, but I want to draw your attention first of all to what is missing from the top. Your brand North Star sits here. Everything ladders to this.

Then, crucially, comes what's often called the spine. I've often seen the customer journey split across 13, even 20 sections or stages as we called them. I think that becomes unwieldy, if only because ultimately you need to use this common language both across the C-suite to get budget, but also from your operational or customer-facing colleagues to get buy-in. In the end, a well-designed map also helps to get understanding and buy-in. By the way, this spine will, of course, vary by industry and brand.

If you're going to use this, I'd also urge you to assert the discipline of having one spine that's used across all of your products, or geographies, or however you use mapping. Make sure that that spine is common to all.

So you've got this common spine across the business. You grab a cross-business group of people, people from retail operations, customer service, HR, Finance and Marketing, in the same room (physical or digital) with a big pile of doughnuts (physical works best here I can assure you). People who know what's really happening in those parts of the business come down and say, 'You know what, this is how our customers see us'. These are individuals and teams that are really connected to your customers.

Now what's also key here is the left-hand side. Remember what we are trying to understand is what the customer is trying to do during this stage of the journey from both a mindset perspective (Do they want to be informed? Do they want to evaluate?) and also what are they doing to achieve this in practice. Are they visiting your website or are they in the store for example? So, what is the customer doing, thinking, feeling?

At a broad level the customer may be:

Researching – Doing,

Confused – Feeling,

Wondering how to get help – Thinking.

From a brand perspective we can slot in our view of what our role is. In the example above, it's about providing help, or education.

I would go into any customer journey mapping sessions with these things already mapped out ready to be explained and worked on.

You now have all your key stakeholders in a room with the 'anatomy' mapped out.

Give them all sticky notes and say, 'Let's now write down the individual points at which we touch customers, from the moment they become aware of us, left to right essentially, from the customer's perspective. All the possible points where you touch your customers or they touch you.' Yes, these are the infamous touchpoints everyone talks about. And, doing this left to right, what you've now built effectively is a sequence map of all the possible points where customers might engage with you. You can use the same approach with colleagues and the same approach with partners. You build a map from their perspective of what you do for them. This is a very powerful tool because it begins to unleash a realisation of what we can do better for the customer. But that's how you start to build the map.

Our role is to gather all this information with a view to understanding what works and what does not work. What are the common pain points or opportunities to deliver more delight?

So, at the end of the session, you now have a column of sticky notes under each stage of the customer journey. But we're not done with sticking yet!

Each team member now gets some red and green dots. They apply a red dot to an area where they think we let the customer down in some way. The green dot is where they think we excel. You should also capture why they are saying this.

You now have improvement areas to focus on but also areas where you're really good that you might also want to focus on and communicate to customers and employees. From my perspective it allows an understanding of the opportunities but also starts the conversation around what the blockers are. Is it a lack of data? Is training required? Is it a technology issue?

The other thing you do, depending on how you've collated this physically, is to get each of the contributors to put their signature on the map. No need for blood, ink will do.

A couple of caveats.

Nothing is allowed to stay on the final version without some kind of qualification. Personal views need to be substantiated. So make sure each important friction or high point is backed up with data. The data could come from:

Voice of customer programmes

CRM data

Brand tracking

Social media

Product reviews

Digital data

No team is allowed to opt out! Total buy-in across the organisation is needed. So ask the original contributors if anyone has been missed.

The voice of the customer has to be represented! And indeed, it might be an opportunity for you take some of the findings and play them back to small groups of customers for validation.

The next stage is to take all these sticky notes, the highs and the lows, and translate them into opportunities – where can we be better or indeed how might we make the most of our high points?

By the way, if you want to excel in front of the customer you might want to consider the neutral points as well. How can you turn them into smiles?

How have Customer Journey maps helped me?

1 – Working with BT, we were able to understand the friction points for new subscribers to its TV and broadband services. We were able to identify where communications could help, resulting in a reduction in both calls to the call centre and lost customers.

2 – With Barratt Homes it helped us understand what point in the buyer's journey was the best time to suggest booking a visit to a development, increasing conversion rates.

3 – Aesop's new customer Welcome Programme delivering 'how to use' content increased customer return rate as well as cementing the relationship between store and customer, ensuring buy-in from the retail teams.

Top 10 Tips

Which customers am I going to focus on? – It's OK to start generic.

What journey will I focus on? Again, its OK to start big and create the template.

What's the anatomy of the journey map, in particular the spine?

Think touchpoints not channels to start with.

What are customers doing, thinking, feeling at that moment?

What's the composition of the cross-functional team?

Sticky notes are your best friend!

What data do I have to support the highs and lows?

Customer validation is important but shouldn't be seen as a reason to delay.

The value is derived from the process and not just the outcome.

It's about using the outcomes to build customer trust – without trust I'm not convinced loyalty will flourish.

Lots of examples can be found here: https://www.pinterest.co.uk/gianfrancocuzziol/customer-journey-maps/

Bayes' Theorem

Developed in the 1740s by the French mathematician Thomas Bayes, the rule, commonly known as Bayes' Theorem, provides a mathematical framework explaining how to revise or update existing beliefs or hypotheses in the light of new evidence or information. Initially, this concept, which was somewhat abandoned by Bayes himself, stirred considerable controversy in the scientific and philosophical communities. The primary reason for the debate was its implication that one could commence with a seemingly arbitrary guess or hypothesis and then progressively refine and adjust this initial belief as additional data or evidence became available.

This approach, while initially viewed with scepticism, laid the groundwork for what is now a fundamental principle in statistical reasoning and scientific method. It underscores the importance of flexibility in thought processes, allowing for the modification of beliefs as new, more compelling information is uncovered. This principle resonates with contemporary business strategies as well.

A notable proponent of this flexible mindset is Jeff Bezos, the founder of Amazon. Bezos upholds the belief that one of the key aspects of always being 'right' or successful in decision-making is the capacity to adapt one's thinking frequently. He is an advocate of the willingness to change one's mind when faced with new evidence or better arguments, emphasizing that this adaptability is crucial for staying relevant and making effective decisions in a rapidly changing business environment. This philosophy, drawing parallels to Bayes' Theorem, highlights the significance of being open to new information and being prepared to alter preconceived notions or strategies in response to evolving circumstances and knowledge.

On Average Switzerland is Flat

And other occasions when the information being used has distorted the outcome

---

Statistically speaking, 50% of people don't find true love.

Thankfully, I've been happily married for 12 years. Unfortunately, my wife hasn't!

The Great Hanoi Rat Massacre

In the depths of Hanoi's colonial era, a rat crisis of epic proportions gripped the city. The scurrying rodents were running rampant, wreaking havoc on public health and turning sanitation into a distant dream. The French colonial authorities, with their characteristic flair for problem solving, devised a cunning plan and the Great Hanoi Rat Massacre was born.

To ignite the fire of enthusiasm among the locals, the authorities dangled a tempting carrot – well, technically, a bounty of one cent per rat. But here's the catch: they only required the submission of a rat's tail to the municipal offices. After all, one can only stomach so many rat corpses before the smell becomes unbearable and spoils the delicate ambiance of a colonial city hall.

Initially, things seemed to be going swimmingly. Rats' tails poured into the collection centres like there was no tomorrow. The French patted themselves on the back, confident in their entrepreneurial ingenuity. Little did they know that their plan was about to take a tailspin. I was going to use the line 'a twist in the tale' but thought better of it.

Enter the enterprising Vietnamese rat hunters, who quickly realised that killing a rat was a double-edged sword. Sure, it earned them a quick reward, but it also meant diminishing the future windfall. They had a stroke of genius – a rat's tail is a rat's pride, so why not keep them alive and kicking? The hunters skilfully became tailors of sorts, snipping off tails with surgical precision and releasing the rats back into the wild. Talk about a rat conundrum!

But wait, there's more! Word got out that some mischievous Vietnamese individuals were smuggling rats into Hanoi from distant lands. Yes, it seemed the city had become a haven for rat refugees seeking a better life, or rather, a better tail. The French authorities surely did not foresee this twist in the plot.

To add a touch of absurdity , French health inspectors stumbled upon rat farms sprouting up in the countryside. These peculiar 'tail creation factories' were churning out rats with precision, breeding them solely for their magnificent tails. Who knew rats had become a hot commodity in the rat-tail fashion industry?

As the chaos unfolded, the French authorities finally faced the music. Their grand plan had backfired spectacularly. Rather than solving the rat problem, they had inadvertently spawned a rat revolution, with cunning hunters and smugglers and even fashion-forward rat farms. It was time to call off the bounty programme, admitting defeat in the face of tail–chopping ingenuity.

The Great Hanoi Rat Massacre, an ambitious endeavour filled with unintended consequences, reminds us that even the most well-intentioned plans can go awry. So, the next time you find yourself facing a rat infestation, remember the cautionary tale of Hanoi – a tale of tails gone wrong, where entrepreneurialism took an unexpected turn down a rat-infested alley.

Sherlock Holmes Goes Camping

Holmes and Watson are on a camping trip. In the middle of the night, Holmes wakes up and gives Dr. Watson a nudge.

'Watson look up into the sky and tell me what you see.'

'I see millions of stars.'

'And what do you conclude from that, Watson?'

Watson thinks for a moment. 'Well,' he says, 'astronomically, it tells me that there are millions of galaxies and potentially billions of planets. Astrologically, I observe Saturn is in Leo. Horologically, I deduce that the time is approximately a quarter past three. Meteorologically, I suspect we will have a beautiful day tomorrow. Theologically, I see God is all-powerful, and we are small and insignificant. Uh, what does it tell you, Holmes?'

'Watson, you idiot! Someone has stolen our tent!'

The Hanoi story is an example of how setting the wrong measure can ultimately be counterproductive. It instigated action based on the 'What gets measured gets done' hypothesis. But we all know that regular measurement and reporting keeps an organisation and individuals focused – because they use that information to make decisions to improve their results. These critical measurements are those blessed Key Performance Indicators (KPIs) we often get asked to report on.

One of the dilemmas we have is finding the balance between what we know to be the long term KPIs and the shorter term results that are required by senior management. Business is not the only area to suffer here.

This is a common criticism of political systems, particularly in democracies where elected officials are typically in office for a relatively short period.

Politicians often focus on short-term fixes because of electoral pressures. In order to be re-elected, they need to show results within their term in office, which is usually a few years. Consequently, they may be incentivised to prioritise immediate benefits over long-term sustainability.

This pattern of focusing on short-term fixes can lead to a cycle of unresolved issues and repetitive, band-aid solutions. It can undermine sustainable policy making, which is critical for issues like climate change, long-term economic growth, healthcare and education, where effects might not be immediately visible but can have far-reaching consequences.

Various reform measures could be introduced to change this scenario:

– Longer Term Limits: Increasing the term length might give politicians more time to implement long-term policies and see them come to fruition.

– Public Education: By increasing public understanding of policy issues, voters can be more appreciative of politicians who champion long-term solutions.

– Performance Measures: Introducing performance measures that take into account long-term outcomes can help realign the incentives for politicians.

– Encouraging Cross-party Collaboration: Some issues are so long-term they need to be addressed beyond the scope of any one party or term. Encouraging parties to work together on these issues could potentially lead to more sustainable outcomes.

It's also important to note that there are valid reasons why politicians focus on short-term issues. Some problems need immediate attention and delay might result in deteriorating conditions. Also, in a rapidly changing world, what seems like a viable long-term solution today might not be relevant or effective in a few years.

Furthermore, politicians also serve as representatives of the people's immediate concerns. In some cases, addressing these concerns might mean prioritising short-term solutions.

While the short-term focus of politicians is often criticised, it's a complex issue embedded in the design of democratic systems and societal expectations. It's crucial to balance immediate needs with long-term sustainability. This requires structural changes in the political system and a shift in public perception.

Yet, the tension between short-term and long-term goals isn't exclusive to politics; it's also a fundamental challenge in marketing and business strategy. Here's how it typically plays out:

1. Short-term Marketing: These efforts aim to drive immediate results, such as a spike in sales, increased website traffic or immediate brand recognition. They typically include promotions, sales events, pay-per-click advertising and other forms of direct-response marketing. The advantage is that results can be measured quickly, providing quick wins and immediate return on investment. However, these effects can be fleeting and may not contribute to long-term brand loyalty or growth.

2. Long-term Marketing: These strategies aim to build sustainable competitive advantages and long-term customer relationships. They can include brand building, content marketing, search engine optimisation (SEO),

public relations and customer relationship management (CRM) initiatives. The payoff for these strategies is often slower and less immediately tangible, which can make them harder to justify in terms of immediate ROI. However, they're crucial for sustainable growth and customer retention.

Balancing these two types of marketing is a significant challenge for many organisations. A focus on short-term results can come at the expense of long-term growth, but neglecting short-term results can lead to immediate financial difficulties and lack of resources for long-term initiatives.

Several factors can influence the balance between short-term and long-term marketing.

– Organisational Culture and Leadership: Companies with a culture and leadership that value long-term growth may be more willing to invest in long-term strategies.

– Market Conditions: In a highly competitive market or during a downturn, companies may feel pressured to focus on short-term wins to survive.

– Budget: Larger organisations with bigger budgets may be able to afford both short-term campaigns for immediate revenue and long-term strategies for sustainable growth.

Just like in politics, finding the right balance between short-term and long-term strategies is crucial for sustainable success. It requires a careful analysis of the organisation's goals, market conditions and available resources.

Several key themes have helped me over the years.

KPIs

The number of Key Performance Indicators (KPIs) a business should have is not set in stone and can vary widely depending on the size of the business, its industry and its strategic objectives. However, the key is to focus on quality over quantity. It's important to choose KPIs that are meaningful and directly tied to strategic business goals.

As a general rule of thumb, many organisations find it effective to focus on around 5-10 KPIs. This is a manageable number that allows for a comprehensive view of performance without becoming overwhelming.

Keep in mind that it's often beneficial to have a mix of high-level KPIs to monitor the overall health and direction of the business, as well as more granular KPIs to track specific operational processes or departmental performance.

Remember that KPIs are not set in stone. They should be reviewed regularly and updated as necessary to ensure they remain aligned with evolving business goals.

So, while there's no definitive number, the key is to focus on a small, manageable number of meaningful KPIs that give an accurate and comprehensive view of your business performance.

Hierarchy

The notion of blending high-level and granular KPIs is worth considering. I've often employed the pyramid structure when building out KPIs.

KPI hierarchy

The pyramid should give a sense that the higher the position in the pyramid the:

more strategic the KPI

less of them there are

less frequently they get reported.

The pyramid should highlight two areas that are commonly missed.

1 – The lower levels act as foundations for the KPIs further up the pyramid.
2 – To ensure a solid pyramid, the blocks are not just added on top of each other but are indeed linked together.

Ensuring that the indicators are linked is crucial. I've often highlighted the problem we spotted when working with a TV broadcaster in the UK whose marketing team wanted to deliver 'hyper' personalised content, not only wanting to reflect the TV and sports package their subscribers were on, but also specific sports and the individual club level. Thus they wanted to speak to customers as TV and sport subscribers who watched football but were also Liverpool fans. This had two drawbacks. Firstly, the subscribers had not come to the broadcaster because of the fact that Liverpool games were being shown but were there because of the breadth of sports coverage. And more pertinently for this perspective, the organisation had set itself top of the pyramid KPIs around customer satisfaction based on the breadth of content being shown to subscribers. So here were the marketing teams actually not giving customers what they wanted, but taking action in direct contrast to what the organisation was trying to achieve!

One KPI to Rule Them All

While managing Manchester United, in 2001 Sir Alex Ferguson made a controversial decision to sell Jaap Stam, a Dutch defender, to Lazio. The story goes that this decision was at least partially influenced by statistics indicating a reduction in Stam's performance.

The story is often quoted in discussions about the use of data in football. It is said that the Manchester United coaching staff noticed a decrease in Stam's 'tackles per game' statistics and interpreted it as a sign of declining performance. Given that Stam was still considered one of the best defenders in the world at the time, this decision was met with surprise and criticism.

Stam then went on to have continued playing success with Lazio in the eternal city of Rome.

However, others argue that the decrease in tackles was not necessarily indicative of reduced performance. Instead, it could have suggested that Stam's positioning and reading of the game were so good that he didn't need to go in for as many tackles. Moreover, this incident is often cited as an example of how data can be misinterpreted or misused.

Manchester United bought Jaap Stam from Dutch club PSV Eindhoven in 1998 for a fee reported to be around £10.6 million, which was a record for a defender at the time.

When Manchester United sold Stam to Lazio in 2001, the transfer fee was reportedly around £16.5 million. The exact amounts can vary based on different sources owing to undisclosed fees and potential add-ons.

It's worth noting that despite the profit on paper, Ferguson later admitted that selling Stam was a mistake, which is often seen as an implicit acknowledgment of the flawed decision-making process.

However, it should be noted that while the statistics narrative is widely shared, the full story behind Stam's sale is likely to involve other factors as well, including possible tensions with Ferguson because of controversial comments in Stam's autobiography. The decision might not have been based solely on performance statistics.

As is often the case in football, decisions like these can be complex and multifaceted. The same as in your business, no doubt.

The misinterpretation or over-reliance on a single statistic without considering a broader context is not unique to football. It happens across many domains, from business to public policy. It's commonly known as 'silo thinking' or 'tunnel vision', and it often leads to poor decision making.

Here are a few examples.

1. Baseball: In the early days of using metrics, baseball scouts and executives would often overvalue batting average without considering other metrics. Batting average only reflects a player's success in getting hits, and not their ability to get on base in other ways (like walks), their power (extra-base hits), or their speed (stealing bases). This overemphasis on batting average led teams to overlook players who could contribute significantly in other ways, leading to suboptimal roster construction.

2. Business: In the business world, companies sometimes focus too heavily on short-term revenue growth without considering the sustainability of that growth. For instance, if a company's revenues are growing because of aggressive price cutting, that might not be sustainable in the long term, and could even lead to a loss of profit. Thus, focusing solely on revenue growth without considering profit margins or customer retention can lead to bad strategic decisions.

3. Healthcare: In healthcare, there can be an overemphasis on certain metrics at the expense of others. For example, prioritising the reduction of waiting times in emergency departments can sometimes lead to rushing patients through the system, resulting in lower quality care or inadequate follow-ups.

These examples illustrate the importance of considering a wide range of factors and using a balanced set of metrics when making decisions. Over-reliance on a single statistic without a wider context can lead to significant missteps.

Three statisticians went out hunting and came across a large deer. The first statistician fired, but missed, by a metre to the left. The second statistician fired, but also missed, by a metre to the right. The third statistician didn't fire, but shouted in triumph, 'On average we got it!'

A Balanced View

The balanced scorecard is a performance measurement framework that provides a balanced view of an organisation's performance by considering a range of different performance measures, not just financial ones. It was introduced by Robert Kaplan and David Norton in the early 1990s.

The balanced scorecard typically looks at an organisation's performance in four areas:

1. Financial Performance: Traditional measures like revenue, profit, return on investment, etc.
2. Customer: Measures of customer satisfaction, loyalty and retention.
3. Internal Processes: Measures of productivity, efficiency, quality, etc.
4. Learning and Growth: Measures of innovation, employee satisfaction and knowledge management.

Perspectives

Internal	Learning & Growth	Customer	Financial
Operational Excellence	Motivated Workforce	Delight the Customer	Increased Revenues
↓	↓	↓	↓
Reduced Inventory	Employee Survey	Customer Satisfaction	Sales

Balanced Scorecard

Example [16]

Here are three pros and three cons of balanced scorecards.

Pros

1. Holistic View: By incorporating a range of measures, the balanced scorecard provides a more comprehensive view of an organisation's performance than financial metrics alone.

2. Alignment with Strategy: The balanced scorecard helps align day-to-day work with the organisation's strategic objectives. By linking individual and team performance measures to the organisation's overall goals, it helps ensure everyone is working towards the same objectives.

3. Focus on Future Performance: The balanced scorecard includes forward-looking measures in the learning and

---

16 Adapted from *The Visual MBA* by Jason Barron.

growth perspective, encouraging investment in future performance, not just short-term results.

Cons

1. Complexity: Implementing a balanced scorecard can be complex and time-consuming. Selecting the right measures, collecting the data, and ensuring they are used effectively for decision making can be a significant undertaking.

2. Subjectivity: While financial measures are objective and straightforward to measure, the other perspectives can involve more subjective measures. There can be disagreement about how to measure things like customer satisfaction or employee morale.

3. Risk of Overemphasis on Measurement: There's a danger that the organisation becomes too focused on meeting the measures in the scorecard at the expense of other important things that might not be so easily measured. This is sometimes referred to as 'hitting the target but missing the point'.

In conclusion, while the balanced scorecard has its limitations, it can be a powerful tool for aligning an organisation's performance with its strategy and providing a more comprehensive view of that performance.

The idea behind the balanced scorecard can be used even in your day-to-day thinking.

Let's take a very simple example such as a new Welcome Journey you've created for customers who have made their first purchase with you. The balanced scorecard approach might view the results in this way.

1. Financial Performance: How much revenue is being generated from the programme?

2. Customer: What is the level of customer satisfaction from customers who go through the journey or perhaps even, depending on your business model, how many customers go on to make a subsequent purchase as a result of the journey?

3. Internal Processes: How easily and quickly can elements of, say, the email content be changed by the local marketing teams to enhance the customer experience?

4. Learning and Growth: How can you put in place measures that highlight innovation, employee satisfaction and knowledge management?

Don't fall into the trap of measuring:

what's easy to measure – that simple-to-get-to number may not be what is actually important (email opens – boring!),

the simple when the outcome is complicated – back to the one KPI to rule them all – life's not that simple (email opens – even more boring!),

standardised metrics across an organisation – although tempting, as it seems as though you have created a common way of measuring performance, you often end up stripping out context and the nuances of different lines of business (email opens – I'm now asleep).

Goodhart's Law

'Any observed statistical regularity will tend to collapse once pressure is placed upon it for control purposes.'[17]

---

17   https://en.wikipedia.org/wiki/Goodhart%27s_law

Or essentially, when a measure becomes a target, it stops being a good measure.

Two real-life examples of where this manifested itself in my career have been in social media and email marketing.

The shipping giant Maersk had an ambition to position itself as a champion of trade in a global economy where, at the time (c. 2016), shipping represented 90% of global trade. As an organisation, it wanted to use social conversations with global influencers and decision makers. So, having a large social following was important and its strategy was tailored to growing this number and they were successful in doing this. An in-depth analysis of this by my analytics team highlighted the fact that what they were actually doing was creating content to pander to a global shipping enthusiast audience. Some people just liked big ships!

Their resources had been focused on quantity rather than quality. So by simply focusing on understanding the real audience they wanted to influence and creating content tailored around their conversations, they were able to cement relationships with global influencers and create partnerships with key bodies.

A global TV and sport broadcaster was obsessed with the open and click-through rates for one of its weekly newsletters. Now don't get me wrong, these metrics are important but if they become the measure of success and resources are dedicated to improving them without any real thought for the longer-term goal, it can be quite distracting. (It actually reminds me of a conversation I had with the Head of CRM at a large retail bank where he literally asked me why I thought two subject lines brought about differing open rates: 'Important banking information enclosed' versus 'Win Free tickets to the

O2'.) In fact, changing the open rate of an email can be easily manipulated, but without looking at the point of the email it is just a case of vanity metrics.

When challenged about the point of the newsletter, where no selling took place, it became apparent that it was there to influence (reduce) churn rate. But no effort had been made to understand the link, if any, between email metrics and churn rate. Why? Because it was deemed to be too hard. As a result, an 'urban myth' was spread that improving open rates would reduce the likelihood of a customer switching to a competitor.

The agency was then let off the hook and simply delivered a test-and-learn or optimisation programme to deliver on those numbers.

At some point, however, someone internally is going to ask the difficult question. Can you prove the link between engagement and churn rate improvement?

I always felt that it was our responsibility to head off these questions early and make it easier for the client to answer that question when finance came knocking. Any agency will suggest engagement but only the good ones will link it to business value. And that's what we did. We put some resources into looking at the numbers and showed that engagement with the content had a positive impact on product usage, brand perception, advocacy and churn rate. Funny what you get with a little bit of effort.

Augie Ray, a Gartner customer-experience analyst, wrote marketers 'must stop overvaluing what is easy to measure and recognise that what's hard to measure is frequently more powerful. Easy measures are important but not predictive of future success'. Or has the Harvard Business Review puts it when talking abo the traps of performance measurement, spending too much time looking backward.[18]

So how does a metric become valuable? Here are some rules.

1 – Metrics are understood by the target audience

The variables you're measuring need to make sense to the people collecting the data and analysing the data, and to those using them for decision making. If metrics are too complicated or convoluted, they probably won't be that useful. It's also worth creating standard definitions of what each metric is so that there can be a common understanding across the business. Don't think you can't be very explicit with those definitions. Defining the meaning, the calculations and time periods involved as well as the source data can be crucial.

2 – Metrics are reliable and can be replicated

Galileo said that a scientist's job was to measure what was measurable and to render measurable what was not.[19] The latter can often prove difficult, let alone trying to work out something that's important but no one has ever measured before. In both instances we need to make sure that we (and more importantly the recipient of the metric) trust the data, its source and that there are no other factors that might influence the numbers.

3 – Metrics are actionable and relevant

Improving the number has a customer and business impact. It's in your remit to impact.

---

18 https://hbr.org/2009/10/the-five-traps-of-performance-measurement
19 Allegedly not said by Galileo but you've probably never heard of the guys who actually said it: https://en.wikiquote.org/wiki/Galileo_Galilei#Quotes_about_Galilei

Sometimes metrics, although seemingly important, are often difficult to impact. Some work with a leading insurance comparison site led to continuous incremental growth on the key metric we were tasked with improving: the 'Click to Quote' number. In essence, a chain of metrics on the email programme that included Opens, Clicks, Quotes.

As an agency we were always pushing back on the Quote figure. We controlled the data, creative, timing of the communications (so opens and clicks we were comfortable with), but we had no control over the landing page performance!

A police officer sees a drunken man intently searching the ground near a lamppost and asks him what he is looking for. The drunk replies that he is looking for his car keys, and the officer helps for a few minutes without success. Then he asks whether the man is certain that he dropped the keys near the lamppost.

'No,' is the reply. 'I lost the keys somewhere across the street.' 'Then why are you looking here?' asks the surprised and now annoyed officer. 'The light is much better here,' the intoxicated man responds.

Ultimately, you'll need to deliver outcomes that find the natural balance in this rather philosophical question:

Is your focus to help customers or is it to help customers buy more from you?

Those metrics might include:

Business	Customer
ROI	Net Promotor Score (NPS)
Cost Savings	Customer Satisfaction (CSAT)
Revenue	Advocacy Rate
Retention	First Call Resolution
Customer Lifetime Value	Return Rate (products)

In general, your CFO is on the left, the CMO on the right.

Read the small print.

An interesting piece of research from the *British Medical Journal.*

Abstract

Objective: To determine if using a parachute prevents death or major traumatic injury when jumping from an aircraft.

Design: Randomized controlled trial.

Setting: Private or commercial aircraft between September 2017 and August 2018.

Participants: 92 aircraft passengers aged 18 and over were screened for participation. 23 agreed to be enrolled and were randomized.

Intervention: Jumping from an aircraft (airplane or helicopter) with a parachute versus an empty backpack (unblinded).

Main Outcome Measures: Composite of death or major traumatic injury (defined by an Injury Severity Score over 15) upon impact with the ground, measured immediately after landing.

Results: Parachute use did not significantly reduce death or major injury (0% for parachute v 0% for control; $P>0.9$). This finding was consistent across multiple subgroups. Compared with individuals screened but not enrolled, participants included in the study were on aircraft at significantly lower altitude (mean of 0.6 m for participants v mean of 9146 m for non-participants; $P<0.001$) and lower velocity (mean of 0 km/h v mean of 800 km/h; $P<0.001$).

Conclusions: Parachute use did not reduce death or major traumatic injury when jumping from aircraft in the first randomized evaluation of this intervention. However, the trial was only able to enrol participants on small stationary aircraft on the ground, suggesting cautious extrapolation to high altitude jumps.

When beliefs regarding the effectiveness of an intervention exist in the community, randomized trials might selectively enrol individuals with a lower perceived likelihood of benefit, thus diminishing the applicability of the results to clinical practice.

Hopefully you read the abstract all the way through to the end. If you didn't and just looked at the overall results you may have missed the line 'However, the trial was only able to enrol participants on small stationary aircraft on the ground'.

It's easy to be hoodwinked into not looking at the detail.

The Cocktail Party

Imagine yourself at a bustling soirée, surrounded by a melange of conversations. Voices intermingle with the clinking of glasses, while the subtle background music adds an additional layer of complexity to the auditory landscape. Yet, amidst this overwhelming din, you are able to focus on a single conversation. How is this possible?

In a world filled with unending cacophony, it is remarkable how the human mind is able to selectively tune into a single conversation at a crowded cocktail party. This phenomenon, known as the 'cocktail party effect', was first introduced by British scientist Colin Cherry in the 1950s. Cherry's insights into auditory perception, attention and cognitive processing have had far-reaching implications in various fields, from psychology to neuroscience and even technology.

Cherry's experiments sought to unravel the mystery behind our ability to attend selectively to one conversation in a sea of voices. In one of his most well-known experiments, he presented listeners with two simultaneous auditory streams – one in each ear – and instructed them to focus on just one of them. Remarkably, the subjects were able to do so with relative ease, demonstrating the power of our attentional mechanisms in the face of competing auditory stimuli.

The cocktail party effect, however, is not without its limitations. While we can effectively filter out irrelevant noise, our attention can be easily hijacked by salient stimuli, such as hearing our own name. This involuntary shift in attention, known as the 'cocktail party phenomenon', underscores the delicate balance between focus and distraction in our cognitive processes.

The implications of Cherry's cocktail party effect extend beyond the realm of auditory perception. In today's world, we are inundated with information from various sources – television, the internet, smartphones, and more.[20] As we navigate through the deluge of information, our ability to focus on what is relevant becomes increasingly crucial. The cocktail party effect offers a metaphor for how we selectively attend to and process the vast amount of information in our daily lives.

Furthermore, Cherry's work has inspired advancements in technology, specifically in the field of audio processing. In recent years, there has been a surge in the development of noise-cancelling headphones and smart speakers, which use complex algorithms to isolate and amplify specific sounds. These innovations are a testament to Cherry's pioneering research and the enduring relevance of the cocktail party effect.

Beyond the technological realm, Cherry's work offers valuable insights into the intricacies of human interaction. As a social species, our ability to communicate effectively is paramount, and the cocktail party effect sheds light on how we navigate the complex landscape of interpersonal communication. It underscores the importance of not only listening, but truly hearing one another, and serves as a reminder that our attention is both a gift and a responsibility.

Colin Cherry's cocktail party idea is far more than an intriguing psychological curiosity. It is a window into the incredible capacity of the human mind to selectively attend to and process the vast array of sensory stimuli that inundate our lives. As we continue to grapple with the complexities of our modern world, the cocktail party effect offers a metaphorical compass, guiding us through the maze of information and helping us stay connected to what truly matters.

---

20 Rumour has it that even in terms of marketing messages we are confronted by 10,000 a day!

The Allure of Personalisation: How the Cocktail Party Phenomenon Shapes Modern Marketing Strategies

In the world of marketing, capturing the attention of a target audience has always been the primary objective. As we know from Colin Cherry's work on the cocktail party phenomenon, our attention can be hijacked by salient stimuli, such as the sound of our own name. This involuntary shift in attention presents a tantalising opportunity for marketers to harness the power of personalisation, making their messages resonate on a deeper, more intimate level with consumers.

At its core, personalisation in marketing involves tailoring messages and experiences to cater to the unique preferences, interests and behaviours of individual consumers. The rise of digital technology and data analytics has made personalisation more accessible and sophisticated than ever before. In the age of information overload, personalised marketing strategies have become essential in cutting through the noise and establishing meaningful connections with potential customers.

The cocktail party phenomenon provides a compelling rationale for the effectiveness of personalised marketing. Just as hearing our own name can involuntarily capture our attention in a crowded room, personalised marketing messages can command the focus of consumers amidst the barrage of generic advertisements. By appealing to our innate desire to be recognized and understood, personalised marketing taps into the psychological underpinnings that drive human behaviour.

Consider the ubiquity of personalised recommendations on e-commerce platforms such as Amazon, which curate product suggestions based on an individual's browsing and purchase history. This targeted approach not only enhances the customer experience by reducing the cognitive load of sifting through countless options, but also increases the likelihood of a purchase. As a result, personalisation in e-commerce has become the gold standard for customer engagement and conversion.

Similarly, personalised email marketing campaigns have been shown to significantly outperform generic ones. By using recipient names in subject lines and tailoring content to reflect individual interests, marketers can create a sense of familiarity and relevance that compels the recipient to open and engage with the email. This strategy not only increases open and click-through rates but also fosters brand loyalty by making customers feel valued and understood.

The power of personalisation extends beyond the digital realm as well. In a time when physical retail spaces are increasingly threatened by the convenience and efficiency of e-commerce, bricks-and-mortar stores have an opportunity to leverage personalisation as a means of differentiation. By employing data-driven insights to create tailored in-store experiences, retailers can foster a sense of connection and community that keeps customers coming back.

However, the allure of personalisation is not without its pitfalls. As marketers collect and analyse vast amounts of personal data to craft highly targeted campaigns, concerns about privacy and data security have become increasingly prevalent. To navigate these ethical dilemmas, marketers must strike a delicate balance between creating personalised experiences and respecting consumer privacy.

Moreover, personalisation can sometimes backfire when it becomes too intrusive or overly familiar, making consumers feel uncomfortable or manipulated. In these instances, the cocktail party phenomenon can be a double-edged sword, as the very strategy designed to capture attention can ultimately repel it. This underscores the importance of understanding the nuances of human psychology and maintaining a level of restraint when implementing personalised marketing tactics.

The cocktail party phenomenon offers a compelling framework for understanding the effectiveness of personalisation in marketing. By harnessing the power of salient stimuli and tapping into our innate desire for recognition, personalised marketing strategies can create meaningful connections with consumers and drive engagement in an increasingly noisy world. However, as marketers continue to push the boundaries of personalisation, it is crucial to remember that the delicate balance between attention and intrusion must be respected to ensure the long-term success of these efforts.

The Timeless Art of Connection: How Dale Carnegie's Principles Can Guide Modern Brands in Building Lasting Relationships

Dale Carnegie, born as Dale Carnagey on November 24, 1888, in Maryville, Missouri, was an American author, lecturer and self-improvement guru. Raised in a modest farming family, Carnegie pursued higher education at the State Teachers College in Warrensburg, Missouri. He began his career as a salesman, selling bacon, soap and lard for Armour & Company. Despite his humble beginnings, he possessed an insatiable desire for self-improvement and a keen interest in public speaking.

Carnegie's passion for effective communication led him to develop a course on public speaking at the YMCA in New York City. The course, which aimed to help individuals overcome their fear of public speaking, was an instant success. Recognising the potential for self-improvement education, Carnegie continued to refine his teachings, eventually establishing the Dale Carnegie Institute, dedicated to helping people improve their interpersonal skills and communication abilities.

In 1936, Carnegie published his seminal work, *How to Win Friends and Influence People*, which has since sold over 30 million copies worldwide and remains a beloved classic to this day.

Drawing from his own experiences and the stories of successful historical figures, Carnegie's book offers practical advice on building relationships, navigating social interactions and becoming a more effective leader. It offers timeless wisdom on the art of building and maintaining relationships. His six fundamental principles, when applied to the realm of marketing and brand–customer interactions, can provide invaluable guidance for brands looking to establish authentic connections with their customers. By applying Carnegie's teachings, marketers can create a conversation that resonates deeply with their audience, fostering loyalty and long-term success.

Become Genuinely Interested in Other People.

For brands, this principle translates into truly understanding their customers. By conducting thorough market research and employing tools such as social listening, brands can gain insights into their customers' preferences, pain points and aspirations. Armed with this knowledge, brands can craft personalised marketing campaigns that demonstrate genuine interest in their customers' needs, thereby fostering trust and long-lasting connections.

Smile

In the context of marketing, a 'smile' can be understood as the positive and authentic tone brands adopt when communicating with their audience. Brands that project warmth and approachability are more likely to create an emotional bond with their customers. By maintaining a consistent and friendly tone across all communication channels, brands can create an atmosphere that encourages customers to engage in meaningful conversations.

Remember People's Names

As we've discussed earlier with Cherry's cocktail party phenomenon, our attention is drawn to the sound of our own name. Brands can leverage this psychological insight by addressing customers by name in email campaigns, social media interactions and customer service communications. By doing so, they can convey a sense of personal connection that makes customers feel valued and appreciated.

Be a Good Listener and Encourage others to Talk about Themselves

In today's digital age, social media platforms provide brands with an unparalleled opportunity to listen and engage with their customers. By monitoring and responding to customer feedback, brands can demonstrate their commitment to open and honest dialogue. Furthermore, by inviting customers to share their stories, preferences and experiences, brands can foster a sense of community and belonging that keeps the conversation alive.

Talk in Terms of the Other Person's Interests

Brands must not only understand their customers' interests but also create content that reflects these preferences. This involves crafting engaging and relevant content across various platforms, such as blog posts, social media updates and targeted email campaigns. By tailoring their messaging to align with customer interests, brands can ensure that their communication resonates deeply with their audience, driving engagement and loyalty.

Make the Other Person Feel Important and Do It Sincerely

Finally, brands must strive to make their customers feel important and valued. This can be achieved through thoughtful gestures, such as sending personalised offers, recognising customer milestones and providing exceptional customer service. By consistently demonstrating their appreciation for customers, brands can create a sense of loyalty and foster long-term relationships.

Dale Carnegie's timeless principles offer a roadmap for brands seeking to create authentic and meaningful connections with their customers. By embracing the spirit of these teachings and applying them to modern marketing strategies, brands can keep the conversation with their customers alive, ensuring lasting loyalty and success in an increasingly competitive landscape. From leveraging the power of personalisation, as discussed earlier, to fostering genuine interest and understanding, Carnegie's wisdom serves as a reminder that the foundation of any successful brand–customer relationship is rooted in the art of human connection.

But What is Personalisation?

Dear Amazon. I bought the sink plunger because of a specific need at the time. It was driven by necessity not desire. I do not collect them. It doesn't matter how many times you email me or add them to my homepage, I'm going to think, 'Oh go on! I'll treat myself'

There are many, many definitions and variations on this but here are ones from both an academic, consultancy and my personal perspective.

Academic

Here are a few academic definitions of personalization in marketing, along with different perspectives and focuses.

1. From a customer-centric viewpoint

'Personalization in marketing refers to the act of designing and producing in ways that resonate with customer preferences.' (Chaffey & Ellis-Chadwick, 2016). This definition emphasizes tailoring marketing efforts to individual needs and preferences for a more relevant experience.

2. Highlighting the role of technology

'Personalization is the use of technology and customer information to tailor a particular product to the specific needs of an individual customer.' (Verhoef, Kannan, & Inman, 2010). This definition brings attention to the technological tools and data utilized to achieve personalization.

3. Focused on individual interactions

'Marketing personalization can be defined as the process of treating each customer as an individual and tailoring communications and offerings to their specific needs and preferences.' (Kumar, Petersen, & Sheth, 2010). This definition emphasizes the one-to-one approach and customized communication aspect of personalization.

4. Considering ethical concerns

'Personalization in marketing is the dynamic tailoring of communications and offerings to individual customers by utilizing their data and predicted behaviour, while adhering to ethical and legal considerations.' (Verhoef, 2021). This definition acknowledges the importance of ethical and legal boundaries when employing customer data for personalization.

Consultancy

Although they are less likely to produce a definition but rather an interpretation.

So here are my interpretations of personalisation based on the perspectives and reports from several consultancies.

1. McKinsey & Company

Focus: Building customer loyalty and advocacy through relevant experiences.

Interpretation: Personalization goes beyond tailoring offerings and messages. It involves understanding customer aspirations, anticipating needs and creating a sense of personal connection.

2. Boston Consulting Group (BCG)

Focus: Leveraging data and technology for individual engagement.

Interpretation: Personalization involves using data analytics and marketing automation to deliver highly relevant content, offers and interactions across channels, creating a seamless and personalized journey.

3. Accenture

Focus: Elevating customer experience through hyper-personalization.

Interpretation: Personalization transcends individual interactions. It's about creating a hyper-personalized ecosystem where every touchpoint reflects the customer's unique preferences and context, fostering deeper engagement and brand loyalty.

Gianfranco

It would be remiss of me not to add my own perspective

This is about putting the customer front and centre and helping the customer do what they need to do by combining both customer preferences and choices with data-inferred preferences.

It needs to have a point that combines what I call the HUM Model:

it keeps the customer Happy – now and later

it provides a Unique proposition – or as close as possible to unique for the customer

it makes Money – either now or later.

Without this focus, personalisation is would seem to be an exercise in perhaps having a solution and trying to find a problem to solve.

The phrase I use is:

Personalisation without purpose is pointless.

Does personalisation differ from customisation?

Personalisation and customisation can be similar in that they both involve tailoring products, services or experiences to meet the needs or preferences of individual customers or users. However, there can be some subtle differences between the two terms.

For me, customisation typically refers to the process of allowing customers to actively choose from a set of options to modify a product or service to their liking. For example, in a custom-made clothing store, the customer chooses the type of cloth, colour, design, size and other options. They are making a conscious decision to often 'personalise' their product or experience. Adding your initials to a shirt is customisation.

Personalisation, on the other hand, often refers to the process of tailoring products, services, or experiences based on data and analytics about the user's behaviour, demographics or other characteristics. This process is often performed automatically, and the customer may not be aware of it. For example, a website that shows different content to different users based on their browsing history or location. I would contend that the shirt supplier above would be personalising the customer experience if next time the customer buys a shirt, the initial customisation is then offered as part of the experience.

In a nutshell, customisation is an active choice made by the user, personalisation is a passive process determined by data.

Personalisation v Relevance

If I get a birthday card from my favourite brand, that is personalisation. If it arrives a week after my birthday, it's personalised but not relevant.

Creating a personalisation strategy typically involves several considerations:

1. Define your goals: Start by defining what you hope to achieve through personalisation. For example, you may want to increase customer retention, sales or engagement. This is not just about personalising a cart abandonment email. Remember, personalisation is not the objective. It is a means by which you can service the customer better.

2. Gather data: Collect data on your customers and their behaviour, such as demographics, purchase history, browsing history and feedback, but also understand their explicit choices. What are their communication preferences? What have they told you about their sizing? But remember the adage – actions speak louder than words! Look at what customers do, not just what they say. You could argue that there are two types of data. Data to learn about customers and data to activate for customers.

3. Segment your audience: Use the data you've gathered to segment your audience into groups with similar characteristics or behaviour. For example, you might segment your audience based on demographics, purchase history or browsing behaviour. One of the fundamentals I believe you need to have in place though is Recency, Frequency, Value (RFV) segmentation.

4. Identify opportunities: Look for opportunities to personalise the customer experience based on the segments you've identified. The obvious examples might be to use browsing data to offer personalised product recommendations or use purchase data to offer personalised promotions or discounts. But you need to think bigger here and focus on the 'choke points' you have in your customer journey.

5. Develop a plan of action: Create a plan of action that outlines how you will implement personalisation and which tactics you will use to achieve your goals. For example, you might create a personalised email campaign, or use data to personalise website content or product recommendations.

6. Test and optimise: Test your personalisation tactics and measure their effectiveness using A/B testing, multivariate testing or other methods. Use the data you gather

to optimise your personalisation strategy over time. Everything is about evolution.

7. Evaluate and improve: Continuously evaluate the results of your personalisation strategy and adjust as needed. Use the data collected to improve the accuracy and effectiveness of the strategy.

It's also important to note that personalisation strategy should be in line with the company's overall goals, values and ethical considerations.

During my spell at Aesop, I remember numerous conversations around what data we should be collecting to help make our communications as relevant as possible. Several marketers were keen to collect customer birth dates. In many organisations, birthday wishes are usually sent with an associated offer (Prezzo, free glass of prosecco with your birthday meal. Greggs, a free sweet treat). But the Aesop brand would never be so obvious so why should we collect birth dates? The conversation moved swiftly on.

Just a quick nod to the term 'Hyper-personalisation'.

In general terms, 'hyper' is a prefix that means 'excessive', 'extremely', or 'beyond the normal or average'. It is used to indicate an intensified or exaggerated state or quality. For example, 'hyperactive' refers to someone who is excessively active or restless, while 'hyperbole' is an exaggerated statement or figure of speech. Nobody wants to be labelled hyperglycaemic or hyperactive.

Hyper-personalisation refers to an advanced level of personalisation that goes beyond traditional personalisation techniques. It involves tailoring products, services or experiences to an individual customer's preferences and needs with a high degree of granularity and specificity. Hyper-personalisation utilises advanced data analytics, artificial intelligence and machine-learning techniques to deliver highly targeted and customised experiences to each individual user.

Businesses gather and analyse large amounts of data from various sources such as browsing behaviour, purchase history, social media interactions and demographic information. This data is then used to create individual customer profiles and deliver personalised recommendations, content, offers or interactions in real time.

The aim of hyper-personalisation is to create a seamless and highly relevant customer experience that fosters engagement, loyalty and satisfaction. It goes beyond simply addressing broad segments or personas and focuses on delivering personalised experiences at an individual level, acknowledging and adapting to the specific preferences, context and behaviours of each customer.

In a nutshell it's hard to do and you can often get it wrong, let alone make it pay its way.

During a spell when I was working with a renowned multi-sports broadcaster, its marketing team was very keen to 'hyper-personalise' subscriber communications, not just at sports level but even to football club level.

We collected the relevant information based on customer stated preferences and viewing habits and ran some tests. Engagement bombed! As did their Customer Satisfaction Scores (CSAT) scores.

What they had forgotten to consider was what the customer wanted and why they had signed up in the first place. They had not signed up for specific club content but for the breadth of sports available through the broadcaster. If they had wanted club content they would be signing up for Manchester United TV, Chelsea TV or Leeds United TV (I had to get Leeds a mention as they are my team).

CSAT dropped because one of the questions being asked was, 'How happy are you with the breadth of sports content being made available?'

Focus on the customer. Not on the hype(r)!

How do I prioritise?

In theory most consultants and project managers will steer you towards a prioritisation matrix like the one below where I've included the added dimensions of JFDIs.[21]

This often comes hand-in-hand with a little bit of horse trading with other key stakeholders (Finance, Technology, Retail, Data, Propositions and your boss! The last is another chapter in its own right but that's for another time).

If you try and boil the ocean you won't even have hot water for a cup of tea.

---

21 My proofreader asked me to define JFDIs were. I refused to on the grounds that it may have given this book a PG rating

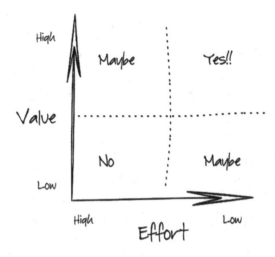

The idea really is to start with what you have. It might just be what the customer bought and where they bought it, if they are a first-time customer.

You might look at those choke points in the customer journey and focus there. The diagram below gives some sense as to what that might look like, say, in the first 30 days of the customer journey. There might be half a dozen opportunities to add value to the business. If you can understand where personalisation will support this, it might be a great way to get going. The priority matrix above will help.

First 30 Day Choke Points

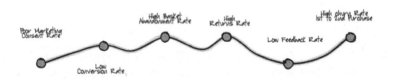

As a quick aside to adding layers of personalisation and customer programmes, I'm amazed by the number or marketers (senior to boot) who feel that the number of automated journeys is a measure of success. A recent brand I worked with boasted of their 180 journeys. When I asked which performed the best and if one journey detracted from another they were less than forthcoming.

I call this CRM Lasagne. Piling on extra layers of ingredients will probably leave you not really knowing where the flavour is coming from. But if you want the best lasagne recipe in the world – read on Macduff! Actually, a misquote of a misquote![22]

---

22 https://wordynerdbird.com/2019/09/18/misunderstood-and-misquoted-shakespeare-lead-on-macduff/

Be Careful What You Wish For

There was once a king in India who was a big chess enthusiast and had the habit of challenging wise visitors to a game. One day a traveling sage was challenged by the king. Having played this game all his life all the time with people all over the world, the sage gladly accepted the king's challenge. To motivate his opponent, the king offered any reward that the sage could name. The sage modestly asked just for a few grains of rice in the following manner: the king was to put a single grain of rice on the first chess square and double it on every consequent one. The king accepted the sage's request.

Having lost the game and being a man of his word, the king ordered a bag of rice to be brought to the chess board. Then he started placing rice grains according to the arrangement: 1 grain on the first square, 2 on the second, 4 on the third, 8 on the fourth, and so on.

Following the exponential growth of the rice payment, the king quickly realized that he was unable to fulfil his promise because on the twentieth square the king would have had to put 1,000,000 grains of rice. On the fortieth square, the king would have had to put 1,000,000,000 grains of rice. And, finally, on the sixty-fourth square, the king would have had to put more than 18,000,000,000,000,000,000 grains of rice, which is equal to about 210 billion tons and is allegedly sufficient to cover the whole territory of India with a metre-thick layer of rice.

It was at that point that the sage told the king that he didn't have to pay the debt immediately but could do so over time. And so the sage became the wealthiest person in the world.

Repeat After Me, 'Data is NOT the New Oil'[23]

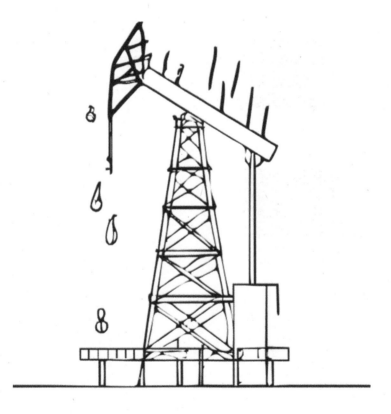

---

23 Technically data is plural so this should read 'Data are not the new oil' but that doesn't match the common usage. I have taken 'data' as singular in this section.

The phrase 'data is the new oil' has become something of a catchphrase in the business and tech worlds over the past few years, as the value and power of data have become increasingly apparent. This saying is a metaphor that likens the place of data in the modern digital economy to the role of oil in the industrial economy of the twentieth century.

What do we mean by oil?

Let's start with a curious paradox. With a name derived from both Greek and Latin – petroleum, or 'rock oil', is born from the very depths of our earth, seeping into cracks and fault lines, finding its way into creeks, ponds and marshes. The word petroleum was first used in 1556 in a treatise published by the German mineralogist Georgius Agricola. Its literal meaning is 'rock oil', from the Latin petra = rock or stone, and oleum = oil. Here, beneath our very feet, was a mystery that for a time was simply an observable fact of nature.

What is the difference between petroleum and oil?

The name petroleum covers both naturally occurring unprocessed crude oil and petroleum products that are made up of refined crude oil. Essentially, while the words petroleum and oil are often used interchangeably, petroleum includes crude oil AND products, while crude oil is just the raw, unprocessed oil itself.

The relationship between humans and oil isn't just a phenomenon of the twenty-first century. No, it's an age-old affair. We can trace its subtle footprints back to ancient civilizations. Picture this: Mesopotamians using this intriguing substance as a bonding agent, an adhesive to piece together their world. The Egyptians, those iconic innovators, utilised pitch to give their chariots that extra smooth glide and asphalt to preserve the eternity of their loved ones.

Now, we must tip our hats to the Chinese. Their ingenuity found underground oil in salt wells. In 600 B.C., Confucius wrote of their depths and in a pioneering approach, they built extensive bamboo pipelines, making the transportation of this new-found elixir a logistical marvel.

Interestingly, for Native Americans oil wasn't about utility alone – it carried a spiritual essence. Imagine painting oneself for a significant ritual using crude oil, setting the stage for a mesmerising dance around ceremonial fires.

And there's a poetic essence to how oil was perceived: as a source of light. There's a certain irony here. The very thing that originated deep in the ground now acted as a beacon to ward off darkness. It was a narrative taken to a dramatic peak by the Romans, who turned oil into fiery projectiles in the heat of battle.

Actually, if there was ever an 'oil central', it would be Azerbaijan. With its name hinting at 'the land of fire', it seemed to be nature's designated hotspot for oil. Spontaneous fires from natural naphtha springs gave rise to a mesmerising sight, compelling the Zoroastrians to establish fire temples that echo through history.[24]

Fast forward to the tenth century on the Absheron Peninsula. The methodology might sound rudimentary, but it was effective. Pits were dug, oil bubbled to the surface and was gathered using simple buckets and pulleys. Oil, in its essence,

---

24   Zoroastrianism is an Iranian religion and one of the world's oldest organised faiths. It is based on the teachings of the prophet Zoroaster.

was diverse; its appearance and texture varied from nearly transparent to the darkest of shades.

The evolution of oil refining began in the thirteenth century. Here we see an interesting transition, where the world once reliant on whale oils for illumination faced an ecological dilemma. As whale populations plummeted, humanity's insatiable thirst led to the brink of several species' extinction.

But as history would have it, innovation came to the rescue. The invention of the kerosene lamp in the 1850s was a game changer. A cleaner form of kerosene, distilled from crude oil, ignited a global hunt for this black gold.

The story of the first modern oil well on the Absheron Peninsula in 1848, the Carpathian mountain wells and the discovery of oil at Oil Creek in Titusville, Pennsylvania, by Edwin Drake are testimonies to humanity's relentless pursuit. The Drake well was symbolic, representing a seismic shift in the American oil industry. Even as I write this in early 2024, the United States is the largest producer of oil in the world.

The rest, as they say, is history. The electric light bulb shifted kerosene out of the spotlight, but petroleum's dance with humanity was far from over. The advent of the automobile transformed gasoline from a mere by-product to the heartbeat of the modern age.

Today, that same oil, once just seeping through earth's cracks, is now the very essence propelling us, defining our journeys and shaping our narratives.

Speaking of Wells

A man stumbles into a deep well and plummets one hundred feet before grasping a spindly root, stopping his fall. His grip grows weaker and weaker, and in his desperation he cries out,

'Is there anybody up there?'

He looks up and all he can see is a circle of sky. Suddenly, the clouds part and a beam of bright light shines down on him.

A deep voice thunders, 'I, the Lord, am here. Let go of the root and I will save you.'

The man thinks for a moment and then yells, 'Is there anybody else up there?'

Hanging by a root has a tendency to tip the scales toward reason.

Here are some reasons why data is often compared to oil.

1. Valuable Resource: Just as oil has been a highly valuable resource due to its wide range of uses in various industries, data is highly valuable in today's economy. Data can be analysed to provide insights, drive decision making, create targeted marketing campaigns, and much more.

2. Needs Refinement: Raw oil needs to be refined before it can be used, and in a similar way, raw data needs to be cleaned, processed and analysed before it can provide value. This requires specialised tools and skills, such as those in data science and data analysis.

3. Availability is Key: Just like oil, data must be available where it needs to be used in the right format at the right time.

4. Fuel for Innovation: Oil powered the industrial revolution and many technological advances. Similarly, data is driving

the information age, powering innovations in artificial intelligence, machine learning, predictive analytics and other advanced technologies.

5. Strategic Importance: Control over oil has historically given nations and corporations significant strategic power. Likewise, entities that control large amounts of data have significant strategic advantages today. This can also raise concerns over data monopolies and data privacy.

6. Economic Impact: Just as economies that managed to harness the power of oil saw tremendous growth and development, economies that are best able to harness the power of data are seeing growth today.

But let's now break it down, focusing on data's role in the world of personalised marketing.

1. Resource Valuation: In personalised marketing, data is the secret sauce that makes everything more appetising. Consider Netflix, which uses viewer data to suggest new shows you might like. Every time you hit 'play', you're contributing to its data reservoir, helping it refine its marketing and serve up the most binge-worthy suggestions. An even better example would be TikTok.

2. Process Refinement: Raw data, like crude oil, needs refining. A data scientist's role is crucial here. Think of the Amazon recommendation engine: it's not magic, it's data science. Behind those 'Customers who bought this also bought ...' messages is a complex process of sorting, analysing and refining vast amounts of purchase and browsing data.

3. Innovation Catalyst: Data fuels the engines of innovation in personalised marketing. Starbucks, for example, uses its rewards app to gather data about customers' buying habits. They use this data to tailor special offers and discounts to

individual users, and even to decide where to open new stores.

4. Strategic Superiority: Data has become a strategic chess piece, just as oil once was. Facebook's ability to offer targeted advertising options is a prime example. Businesses can target their ads to people based on age, location, interests, and much more. The more data Facebook gathers, the more precisely businesses can target their ads, and the more strategic value Facebook holds.

5. Economic Impact: Just as economies leveraging oil experienced growth, those leveraging data are reaping huge benefits. Google Ads is a testament to this. By using data to help businesses reach the right people at the right time, Google has created an advertising empire worth billions.

So, in a way, yes, data is the new oil, especially in personalised marketing. But it's a unique kind of oil. An oil that is intangible yet incredibly powerful, changing the way businesses interact with customers one click at a time.

But while the analogy 'data is the new oil' does highlight the immense potential and value of data in today's economy, it is not a perfect metaphor. Here are a few key reasons.

1. Non-Depletable: Oil is a finite resource; once used, it cannot be replaced. Data, on the other hand, is virtually inexhaustible. Every digital action generates new data, and the same data can be used repeatedly without being depleted. In fact, the amount of data being created is growing exponentially with the advent of new technologies and digital platforms.

2. Non-Rivalrous: Consumption of oil by one party necessarily reduces the amount available for others, making

it a rivalrous commodity. Data, however, is non-rivalrous. Multiple entities can use the same data simultaneously without diminishing its value or availability.

3. Decentralization and Ownership: While oil reserves are geographically specific and their ownership is clear, data can be created and stored anywhere, and its ownership can be ambiguous. This raises complex issues around data privacy, rights and governance.

4. Risk and Ethics: Using oil involves environmental risks like spills and pollution. With data, the risks are more about privacy, security and ethical usage. Misuse of data can lead to breaches of privacy and trust, and the manipulation of individuals or systems.

5. Regulation: Oil production, distribution and usage are regulated by a mature set of laws and standards. On the other hand, the regulation of data is still evolving and varies significantly across countries and regions. There is an ongoing debate around how data should be regulated, who should do it, and what principles should guide these regulations.

6. Value Extraction: To extract value from oil, it needs to be physically processed and refined. For data, the extraction of value is an intellectual process requiring analytical skills and often advanced algorithms and computing power.

So, while data does indeed hold a similar transformative potential as oil once did, its unique characteristics demand different strategies for value extraction, pose different challenges and require a new and evolving set of rules and ethics for its management.

But in today's environment is there a better analogy?

But what if we looked at an organisation's role with customer data. What if we decided to not just think about how we can use the data for our own purposes but also to give something back to the customer? What if we were merely custodians of the data, empowered by our customers to use their data to give back something that has increased in perceived value?

This is a fascinating shift, but one that might just provide a more accurate metaphor could be to venture into a new landscape where 'data is the new soil'.

1. Fertile Ground: The soil is a living, constantly changing ecosystem, full of potential. Similarly, data in its raw form holds immense potential. The role of brands is to till this soil, to work and refine the data, uncovering the fertile layers of insight beneath the surface.

2. Planting Seeds: Once the soil has been prepared, the next step is to plant the seeds – that's your marketing strategy. The seeds might be the same, but the soil (data) changes from place to place, from customer to customer. Understanding the specific data-soil allows for a personalised strategy that is more likely to take root and flourish.

3. Nurturing Growth: Good farmers don't just plant seeds and walk away. They nurture them, feed them and watch them grow. In the data world, this means constantly monitoring and adjusting, based on new data. Your marketing campaigns should be dynamic, adjusting and responding to customer interactions and feedback.

4. Harvesting: Finally comes the harvest. For marketers, this is the conversion – a sale, a subscription, a download. But just as farmers give back to the soil through crop rotation and composting, brands must also give back to the data-soil. This can mean enhancing the user experience or

offering personalised benefits to the consumer. The relationship should be symbiotic, not exploitative.

5. Seasons and Cycles: Just like soil, data is not a static entity. It changes over time and its productivity may wax and wane. Recognising the cyclical nature of data, respecting its seasons and understanding its changing nature is key to sustainable and successful marketing.

However, just as farmers face challenges with changing climates and maintaining the health of their soil, brands also face challenges with data. These include maintaining privacy and ethical standards, securing data to prevent breaches and ensuring that the data-soil isn't overworked or depleted, which could lead to consumer fatigue and distrust.

So, while data may be the new soil for brands, it requires careful, thoughtful cultivation. It's not just about extracting value, but also about nurturing and giving back, creating a healthy, productive and sustainable data environment that benefits everyone involved.

Of course, this level of commitment to a valuable resource demands that we have a strategy in place to deliver this value back to stakeholders. Note the use of the word stakeholder at this point and not just shareholder.

There is a widespread belief in the business world, often supported by various research and articles, that there's a strong link between employee satisfaction and customer satisfaction, which ultimately impacts business success. The general idea is that when employees are satisfied and engaged, they provide better service, leading to more satisfied customers, which can result in better business outcomes.

'Looking into the Service–Profit Chain' introduced in the mid-90s by James L. Heskett, Earl Sasser, and Leonard A. Schlesinger, is a theory that links employee satisfaction and loyalty to customer loyalty and profitability. It's one of the foundational concepts in understanding the link between employee satisfaction and business success.

So, when thinking about data, we need to also bear this in mind.

But What About a Strategy for Data?

Having a clear plan for using data can help a business make more money, increase profits and keep customers happier. This plan gives a guide on how to sort, handle, study and use the data you have. It turns basic data into useful information for making smart choices. More than just powering daily tasks, this plan shows businesses how valuable their data is, almost like treasure, to give the best service to their clients.

The Data Intuition: How Numbers Shape Our Best Choices

Making decisions based on data can assist in recruiting top-notch employees, creating standout products and channelling resources into the most beneficial projects. Numerous sectors can benefit from thorough data analysis. In particular in the customer journey, charting the interactions of your customers with your business allows each interaction point to be seen as a chance to refine and upgrade decision making and improve the customer experience.

Benefits of a Data Strategy
The Safety Illusion: Spotting Shadows Before They Loom Large

Ongoing assessments can identify potential regulatory and security concerns earlier than otherwise. Data tools can spotlight unusual patterns or figures. Relevant team members get instant alerts, enabling them to examine the situation and take necessary rectification measures.

Pennywise Patterns: The Subtle Art of Data-driven Frugality

Data analysis can shape the pricing strategies for offerings. Such analyses can also predict the consequences of diverse pricing structures or payment plans for specific items or tasks. By evaluating data, you can identify and address inefficiencies, whether in manufacturing or software creation. Using data insights within current work structures can enhance efficiency.

Echoes of Loyalty: Listening to the Silent Whispers of Customers

Forecast customer preferences by studying their actions and purchasing habits. Suggest offerings based on their past behaviour. Accumulate feedback to pinpoint prevalent themes that can elevate customer service and overall user experience. Recognize elements that either boost loyalty or lead to customer churn and act on them proactively. Understanding customer profiles can reveal their buying tendencies and personal preferences.

The Message Maze: Navigating the Data-laden Paths of Marketing

Determine the most effective communication channels and messages. Gathering and analysing data lets you distinguish between effective and ineffective strategies, refining your marketing initiatives in the process. Construct marketing summaries and visual representations that provide practical insights for your marketing division. Utilising precise data can merge marketing seamlessly with sales to gauge the impact of marketing on sales figures. Predictive models can forecast business trends, offering a strategic edge.

Ripples in Routine: The Butterfly Effect of Operational Insights

Augment internal procedures by keeping tabs on activities and their causes. Disseminating data insights throughout your organisation can spur overarching enhancements. This ensures that shifts align with overarching business goals, promoting a holistic improvement instead of isolated tweaks.

Objective Laddering

At a meeting of the college faculty, an angel suddenly appears to the head of the philosophy department. 'I will grant you whichever of three blessings you choose: Wisdom, Beauty – or ten million dollars.' Immediately, the professor chooses Wisdom. There is a flash of lightning and the professor appears transformed, but he just sits there, staring down at the table. One of his colleagues whispers, 'Say something'.

The professor says, 'I should have taken the money.'

The Critical Elements of a Data Strategy

1. Vision and Value: Create clear data-driven use cases

Golden Rule

Data Strategy should always align with the overall strategy and business objectives of the business.

Ship: Please divert your course 0.5 degrees to the south to avoid a collision.

Reply: Recommend you divert your course 15 degrees to the south to avoid a collision.

Ship: Negative. You will have to divert your course 15 degrees to the north to avoid a collision. This is the captain of a US Navy ship. I say again, divert YOUR course.

Reply: No. I say again, you divert YOUR course.

Ship: THIS IS THE AIRCRAFT CARRIER USS ABRAHAM LINCOLN, THE SECOND LARGEST SHIP IN THE UNITED STATES' ATLANTIC FLEET. WE ARE ACCOMPANIED BY THREE DESTROYERS, THREE CRUISERS AND NUMEROUS SUPPORT VESSELS. I DEMAND THAT YOU CHANGE YOUR COURSE 15 DEGREES NORTH. THAT'S ONE – FIVE – DEGREES – NORTH, OR COUNTER MEASURES WILL BE UNDERTAKEN TO ENSURE THE SAFETY OF THIS SHIP.

Reply: This is a lighthouse. Your call.

This is not about having data and finding a use for it. Think about what you 'should' be doing as opposed to what you 'can' do. It's about listening to the organisation and its needs and evaluating how data supports that need and the return/feasibility combination.

Crafting clear data-driven use cases as part of an organisation's 'Vision and Value' strategy is pivotal for aligning data initiatives with business objectives and showcasing the tangible benefits of data investments.

Here's what this entails in practical terms.

2.   Framework Definition

Data-driven use cases define scenarios or problems where data analytics or other data-related solutions can provide meaningful insights or solutions, delivering real business value.

Practical Implications

Alignment with Business Objectives

- Understanding Core Objectives: Before creating use cases, it's essential to understand the key goals and challenges of the organisation.

- Identifying Opportunities: Pinpoint areas where data can play a crucial role in providing insights, efficiencies or innovative solutions.

Research and Exploration:

- Data Exploration: Delve into the existing data to discover patterns, anomalies or potential areas of interest.

- Industry Benchmarking: Analyse what competitors or similar industries are doing with their data to identify potential use cases.

Stakeholder Engagement

- Collaborative Workshops: Organise sessions with department heads and teams to understand their challenges and areas where data might assist.

- Feedback Mechanisms: Establish channels for regular feedback to refine and improve upon the proposed use cases.

Use Case Documentation

- Clear Definition: Document each use case with a clear problem statement, data requirements, expected outcomes and business value.

– Prioritisation: Not all use cases will have the same impact or feasibility. Prioritise them based on potential value, resource requirements and strategic alignment.

Prototyping and Testing

– Rapid Prototyping: Develop quick models or solutions to test the validity of the use case.

– Pilot Testing: Before a full scale roll-out, test the use case in a controlled environment or with a smaller audience to gauge effectiveness.

Measurement and Reporting

– Key Performance Indicators (KPIs): Define metrics that will indicate the success of the use case implementation.

– Regular Reporting: Track and report the progress and impact of the data-driven use case to stakeholders.

Iterative Refinement

– Continuous Improvement: As you gather more data and feedback, continuously refine and improve the use case.

– Scalability: Once a use case proves successful in one area or department, consider how it can be scaled or replicated in other parts of the organisation.

For an organisation, focusing on 'Vision and Value' to create clear data-driven use cases means translating abstract data capabilities into tangible actions and outcomes. These use cases serve as a roadmap, guiding teams on how to harness data in ways that align with and further the organisation's overarching goals.

3. Data Management: Define data quality standards, implement data security and privacy measures

Defining data quality standards and implementing data security and privacy measures are critical actions for organisations in today's data-centric world.

Golden Rule

Garbage In: Garbage Out

In practical terms, this means:

Data Quality Standards

Definition: Data quality standards refer to the criteria set by an organisation to ensure that the data they use is accurate, timely, relevant, complete and consistent. This also includes ensuring that data is understandable and that its source is trustworthy.

Practical Implications:

— Data Accuracy: Organisations will need to put checks in place to minimise errors. This might involve validation rules or verification processes.

— Data Timeliness: The data should be updated regularly. For instance, if customer contact information is stored, it needs to be up to date to be of value.

— Relevancy: Data collected should be relevant to the needs of the organisation and not superfluous.

— Completeness: Incomplete datasets can skew analytics and decision making. Measures should be in place to identify and address gaps in the data.

— Consistency: The organisation must ensure that data formats and standards are maintained across different departments and systems.

- Audits: Regular data audits can be carried out to measure the quality of the data against the set standards.

4. Data Security and Privacy Measures

Golden Rule

Treat all data as if it was your own personal information.

Definition: Data security involves protecting data from unauthorised access, data breaches and cyber attacks. Privacy measures ensure that personal data is collected, stored and managed in ways that both comply with legal regulations and respect individual rights.

Practical Implications

- Access Controls: Ensure that only authorised individuals can access certain sets of data. This could involve password protection, multi-factor authentication and role-based access controls.

- Encryption: Encrypt sensitive data both in transit (as it's being transmitted over networks) and at rest (when stored in databases or on disk).

- Backup and Recovery: Back up data regularly to secure locations and have procedures for restoring data in case of loss or corruption.

- Regular Security Assessments: Continuously assess and improve security measures. This can involve penetration testing, vulnerability assessments and more.

- Training: Educate staff about the importance of data security and how to recognize threats like phishing attacks.

- Privacy Policies and Compliance: Ensure that you are aware of regulations like GDPR, CCPA, or other regional data protection laws, and that your data collection and management practices comply with them. This includes providing mechanisms for customers to access, correct or delete their data.

– Incident Response Plan: Have a clear plan in place for how to respond if a data breach does occur. This includes identifying the breach, mitigating damage, notifying affected parties and taking steps to prevent future breaches.

For an organisation, ensuring data quality and implementing stringent data security and privacy measures means investing time, resources and capital. However, in the long run, these investments protect the organisation from costly breaches, regulatory fines and loss of reputation, and ensure that decisions are made based on high-quality data.

5. Technology and Architecture: Develop a data architecture

Golden Rule
Build for now but with the future in mind – think Lego!

Developing a data architecture as a part of an organisation's 'Technology and Architecture' strategy is central to ensuring that data is well organised, accessible, secure and suitable for analysis. Here's what this entails in practical terms.

Framework Definition
Data Architecture refers to the design and structure of data, combining principles, policies, rules and standards that govern the collection, storage, arrangement, integration and use of data in an organisation.

Practical Implications

Infrastructure and Storage

- Centralised v Decentralised Systems: Deciding on whether data should be stored centrally or spread across multiple databases or locations.

- Storage Solutions: Investing in technologies like relational databases, data lakes or cloud storage solutions that align best with the organisation's needs.

Data Models and Design

- Schema Design: Outlining the structure and organisation of data, considering aspects like tables, relationships, keys and indexes.

- Entity–Relationship Diagrams: Designing how different data entities relate and interact with each other.

Integration and Interoperability

- Data Integration: Ensuring data from various sources can be brought together coherently.

- Application Integration: Making sure that different software applications can communicate and exchange data efficiently.

Data Quality and Consistency

- Data Standardisation: Implementing standards to maintain consistency in data entry, naming conventions and formats.

- Data Cleaning: Regular processes to identify and rectify inaccurate or corrupt data.

Scalability and Performance

– Optimisation: Regularly tuning databases and systems to ensure swift data retrieval and transaction speeds.

– Future-proofing: Designing the architecture in a manner that means it can handle future data growth and technology shifts.

Security and Compliance

– Data Access Controls: Setting up permissions to determine who can access specific data and what they can do with it.

– Data Protection Measures: Implementing security protocols, including encryption, to protect data from breaches and unauthorised access.

– Compliance: Ensuring that the architecture adheres to regional and industry-specific data regulations.

Analytics and Reporting

– Reporting Tools: Incorporating platforms or tools that enable effective data visualisation and reporting.

– Real-time Analysis: If applicable, designing the architecture to support real-time data processing and analytics.

Backup and Recovery

– Data Backup Strategies: Implementing regular data backup protocols to prevent data loss.

– Disaster Recovery Plans: Setting up systems to restore data and maintain operations in the event of unforeseen issues or disasters.

For an organisation, focusing on 'Technology and Architecture' to develop a data architecture means ensuring that data is not just stored, but it is also easily retrievable, interpretable, secure and primed for analysis. This requires a blend of the right technologies, methodologies and best practices to manage and utilise the data effectively.

6. Operating Model: A data governance framework

Golden Rule

Empower and enable, not restrict and restrain.

Implementing a data governance framework as part of an organisation's operating model is an approach to formally manage data assets. In practical terms, here's what this means for an organisation.

Framework Definition

Data Governance Framework: This refers to the process, responsibilities, policies, standards and metrics that ensure the efficient and effective use of information in enabling an organisation to achieve its goals.

Practical Implications

a.   Roles and Responsibilities

– Data Stewards: Individuals or teams designated to be responsible for data quality, metadata management and other data-related tasks within specific departments or business units.

– Data Governance Council or Committee: A group of senior leaders and stakeholders who provide guidance, set priorities and make decisions related to data governance.

b. *Policies and Standards*

– Data Classification: Categorize data based on sensitivity (e.g., public, internal, confidential, restricted).

– Data Life Cycle Management: Defining how data is created, maintained, archived and ultimately purged or destroyed.

– Data Quality Standards: As previously mentioned, these ensure data accuracy, consistency, timeliness and relevance.

– Metadata Management: The practice of managing descriptions of data, which helps in understanding the type, use and lineage of the data.

c. *Processes and Procedures*

– Change Management: Implementing processes for changes in data models, databases or other major data shifts.

– Data Access and Usage: Defining who can access what data, under what circumstances and for what purposes.

– Incident Management: Procedures for dealing with data-related issues like breaches, corruption or system failures.

d. *Metrics and Monitoring*

– Key Performance Indicators (KPIs): Monitoring the health and efficiency of data governance initiatives. For example, measuring the percentage of data quality issues resolved within a given time frame.

– Auditing: Regularly reviewing and verifying compliance with data governance policies and standards.

e. *Tools and Technology*

– Data Cataloguing Tools: Software solutions that help in documenting and discovering data across the organisation.

– Data Quality Tools: Software that helps in identifying, correcting and preventing data quality issues.

f. Training and Culture

– Awareness Programmes: Ensuring that everyone in the organisation understands the importance of data governance.

– Training Sessions: Providing staff with the necessary skills and knowledge to adhere to data governance principles and practices.

For an organisation, integrating a data governance framework into its operating model means establishing clear structures, responsibilities and practices around data. It ensures that data is treated as a valuable asset and is managed properly throughout its life cycle. This ultimately leads to better decision making, improved operational efficiency, reduced risks and better compliance with regulations and standards.

7. People and Culture: Build a data analytics capability

Golden Rule

Culture eats strategy for breakfast (although I quite like whipped ricotta, honey and English muffins).

Building a data analytics capability within an organisation's 'People and Culture' strategy involves cultivating a working environment where data-driven decision making is woven into the organisation's ethos. Here's what this entails in practical terms.

Framework Definition

Data Analytics Capability: The capacity of an organisation to gather, process, analyse and interpret data to inform business decisions, strategies and operational improvements.

Practical Implications

Talent Acquisition and Development

- Hiring Data Talent: Recruit data scientists, analysts, data engineers and other data professionals who can contribute technical expertise.

- Continuous Training: Offer regular training sessions and workshops to keep the team abreast of the latest data analytics tools and techniques.

- Cross-training: Train employees from other departments in basic data literacy, ensuring that a greater number of team members can comprehend and utilise data in their roles.

Collaboration and Team Structures

- Data Teams: Forming dedicated teams or units, like a Centre of Excellence, to manage data analytics projects.

- Cross-functional Collaboration: Foster collaboration between data professionals and other departments to ensure insights derived from analytics are actionable and relevant.

Tools, Platforms and Infrastructure

- Investment in Technology: Acquire modern data analytics platforms, tools and infrastructure to support data analysis.

- Data Access: Ensure data is accessible to those who need it, fostering a culture of transparency whilst ensuring data security and privacy.

Processes and Methodologies

- Standardised Analytics Process: Implementing a structured approach to data analysis, ensuring consistency and reliability in insights.

- Feedback Loop: Establish processes to receive feedback on analytics outcomes, aiding in continuous refinement and improvement.

Mindset and Culture

- Promote Curiosity: Encourage employees to ask questions and explore data for insights.

- Data-driven Decision Making: Instil a mindset where decisions are based on data and insights rather than solely on intuition or gut feeling.

- Celebrate Successes: Recognise and reward teams and individuals who make noteworthy contributions through data analytics.

- Encourage Experimentation: Create an environment where employees feel safe to experiment, innovate and occasionally fail, fostering continuous learning.

Ethics and Responsibility

- Data Ethics: Train employees on the ethical aspects of data usage, ensuring data is used responsibly and without bias.

- Data Privacy and Security: Ensure that employees understand the importance of data privacy and security, and they adhere to best practices and regulations.

For an organisation, focusing on 'People and Culture' to build a data analytics capability means more than just hiring the right talent. It's about creating an environment where data is valued and its potential fully realised, and where everyone, regardless of their role, recognises the importance of data in propelling the organisation forward.

8. Roadmap: Create and preserve your advantage

Golden Rule

'It is not the strongest of the species that survives, nor the most intelligent that survives. It is the one that is most adaptable to change.'[25]

Creating and preserving an advantage through a data roadmap as part of an organisation's data strategy is about leveraging data to maintain and enhance the organisation's competitive position. In practical terms, here's what this entails.

Framework Definition

A data roadmap outlines a structured and strategic plan of action focused on utilising data to achieve specific business objectives and sustain a competitive edge over time.

Practical Implications

1. Assessment of Current State

– Gap Analysis: Assess the current data capabilities against desired outcomes to identify areas for improvement.

– Data Audits: Understand what data the organisation already has, where it's stored, and its quality and relevance.

2. Setting Clear Objectives

– Business Goals: Define what the organisation aims to achieve through its data initiatives.

---

25 Just for the record this wasn't actually said by Darwin.

– Key Milestones: Identify significant events or achievements that will indicate progress towards these goals.

3. Prioritisation

– Quick Wins: Identify initiatives that can yield immediate results to build momentum.

– Long-term Projects: Determine initiatives that will take longer but have a significant impact on preserving and enhancing the organisation's advantage.

4. Resource Allocation

– Budgeting: Determine the financial resources required for different initiatives on the roadmap.

– Talent Management: Ensure the organisation has the necessary expertise to execute the roadmap, whether in-house or via external partnerships.

5. Stakeholder Engagement

– Collaboration: Engage various departments to ensure the roadmap aligns with the broader organisational strategy.

– Feedback Mechanisms: Establish channels for consistent feedback from stakeholders to ensure the roadmap remains relevant and effective.

6. Implementation

– Project Management: Ensure that projects on the roadmap are executed on time and within budget.

– Continuous Monitoring: Use analytics and feedback to monitor the success of each initiative, making necessary adjustments as needed.

9. Review and Refinement

– Periodic Reviews: Regularly revisit the roadmap to assess its effectiveness and make any necessary changes.

– Adaptability: As the external business environment evolves, the roadmap should be flexible enough to adapt to new challenges and opportunities.

10. Sustainability and Future Planning

– Continuous Learning: Encourage a culture where the organisation is always seeking to learn from its data initiatives and from the broader industry trends.

– Future-proofing: Ensure that the roadmap takes into account future technological developments and industry shifts, so the organisation remains ahead of the curve.

For an organisation, focusing on the 'Roadmap' to create and preserve an advantage means proactively planning how to use data as a strategic asset. This roadmap becomes the guide for how data will drive the organisation's decisions, innovations and operations, ensuring it remains competitive in an increasingly data-driven marketplace.

Fundamentally the data strategy should result in a 'data flywheel'. This is the nirvana of data strategies. As you start to derive insights from the data and those insights are so valuable and actionable that the customers transact more with you and, as a result, share more with you, that leads to an even richer set of data, and therefore an even more valuable set of insights. And you see that the flywheel happens. Often called 'data network effects', I call it a 'data flywheel'.

Data Flywheel

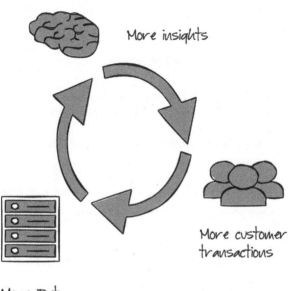

More insights

More customer transactions

More Data

There are two types of people in this world: One, who can extrapolate from incomplete data. Two.

Tailor Made

A man tries on a made-to-order suit and says to the tailor that he needs this sleeve taken in! 'It's two inches too long!'

The tailor says,'No, just bend your elbow like this. See, it pulls up the sleeve.

The man says. 'Well okay, but now look at the collar! When I bend my elbow, the collar goes halfway up the back of my head.'

The tailor says, 'So? Raise your head up and back. Perfect!'

The man says,'But now the left shoulder is three inches lower than the right one!'

The tailor says.'No problem. Bend at the waist over to the left and it evens out.'

The man leaves the store wearing the suit, his right elbow crooked and sticking out, his head up and back. The only way he can walk is with a herky-jerky crooked gait

Just then, two passers by notice him. Says the first 'Look at that poor crippled guy. My heart goes out to him. Says the second: Yeah, but his tailor must be a genius. That suit fits him perfectly!'

Are you fitting solutions to non-existing problems?

The Conversation

In the year 1974, the American consciousness was weighed down by the burgeoning spectre of surveillance. This widespread apprehension permeated the air, spawning an undercurrent of collective anxiety. Remember, the Watergate scandal was the political scandal in the United States involving President Richard Nixon's administration undertaking illegal surveillance activities. This period from 1972 to 1974 led to Nixon's resignation. It was amidst this turbulent climate that Francis Ford Coppola unveiled a masterpiece – *The Conversation*. Not just another cinematic production, this film delved into the intricate complexities of personal privacy, professional ethics and the blurred boundaries of moral dilemmas, striking a chord that has resonated across generations. Hailed by critics and wholeheartedly embraced by audiences, the film carved its niche as an emblematic testament to the era.

Anchoring the narrative within this cinematic marvel is an ensemble cast of seasoned actors, led by Gene Hackman, who plays the role of Harry Caul. Harry, a surveillance expert, is a solitary figure, an enigma in a cheap raincoat. His outward demeanour veils an internal world teeming with profound solitude, an intricate web of professional detachment and personal introspection, and an unspoken burden arising from the moral implications of his occupation. Serving as a counterpoint to Harry's character is Stan, portrayed by John Cazale. More casual in his approach to their line of work, Stan offers an interesting contrast to Harry. The cast also includes a young Harrison Ford as Martin Stett, an integral yet burgeoning talent who adds a sense of menace to the proceedings (although in my opinion he is much better suited to his *Star Wars* and *Raiders of the Lost Ark* outings).

At the heart of the film is a seemingly innocuous conversation, recorded by Harry, taking place in San Francisco's Union Square. A dialogue between a couple, Ann and Paul, that Harry,

The Conversation Poster

despite his usual indifference to the content of his recordings, finds strangely captivating. One line stands out – 'He'd kill us if he had the chance!'. This statement burrows into Harry's psyche, nudging him into the throes of an ethical maelstrom.

Harry is often seen in his 'lab' trying to blend the various recording/data sources to put together the puzzle without a picture as a reference.

Initially, Harry shrugs off the statement as mundane chatter. Yet, something continues to gnaw at him, a burgeoning sense of foreboding. As he immerses himself deeper into the audio recordings, the chilling prospect of potential violence begins to consume him. This isn't merely a line any more; it signifies the harrowing possibility that the subjects under his surveillance could be in mortal peril from the very client paying for that surveillance. This quandary forces Harry onto a tightrope, precariously balancing between professional obligation and personal conscience.

The ethical maze Harry navigates symbolises the profound moral dilemmas inherent in surveillance work. Despite maintaining a facade of professional detachment, Harry is haunted by the spectre of a previous assignment with fatal consequences. The phrase 'He'd kill us if he had the chance' not only amplifies Harry's escalating paranoia but also serves as a catalyst for a journey that wrestles with guilt, introspection and the eventual recognition of the devastating fallout of his actions.

The Conversation transcends the straightforward unravelling of a mystery. It presents a poignant commentary on the dynamics of surveillance, emphasising the inherent power of the observer and the corresponding vulnerability of the observed. It unveils the harsh realities of a profession whose activities can compromise human dignity and violate personal privacy.

Fast forward to the digital age, where the demarcation between physical and virtual privacy is increasingly blurred, and the thematic undercurrents of surveillance within the film become even more pertinent. They reflect the conundrum that underpins today's marketing landscape – the privacy–personalisation paradox. Much like Harry, businesses today find themselves caught in the ethical crossfire of balancing personal privacy against the desire for data-driven customisation.

In essence, the tension inherent in *The Conversation* is emblematic of this paradox. The ominous statement, 'He'd kill us if he had the chance', morphs into a grim warning against the misuse of data, illustrating the catastrophic consequences that can ensue when information falls into the wrong hands. It mirrors the dilemmas faced by businesses, much like Harry's ethical tug-of-war between safeguarding the couple's privacy or fulfilling his professional mandate of handing over the recordings.

Entwined in this intricate narrative, the characters of Ann and Paul further underscore the perturbing exchange, 'He'd kill us if he had the chance'. Their connection to an enigmatic figure, the 'Director', played by Robert Duvall, adds an intriguing dimension to the story. The 'Director' is not a film director, as might be assumed, but a high-ranking official within a corporation or organisation. FBI? CIA? Who knows? His identity is purposefully shrouded in ambiguity, only indirectly connected to Ann and Paul, without any direct interaction, thereby amplifying the mystery that envelops the film.

The 'Director' character commissions the surveillance on Ann and Paul, but his motivations remain murky. Is he a jilted lover, a wary business associate, or a figure of a different nature entirely? The film refrains from providing definitive answers, inviting viewers to form their own interpretations.

This narrative device augments the suspense, highlighting the voyeuristic nature of surveillance and reflecting real-world scenarios where information is often gathered without fully understanding the context.

[**SPOILER ALERT**]

As the plot progresses, the chilling line, 'He'd kill us if he had the chance', experiences a dramatic transformation. Plagued by the potential implications of this statement, Harry's paranoia escalates and he becomes fraught with the fear that he may inadvertently abet a horrific crime by delivering the tape to the Director.

However, a dramatic twist is unveiled when, driven by his obsessive desire to protect Ann and Paul, Harry decides to play the tape again. This time, he notices a change in the inflection, suggesting a shift in the context of the conversation. The line that had haunted him and propelled the narrative isn't a warning of danger from the Director, but perhaps a declaration of intent from Ann and Paul themselves.

This revelation underscores the perils of surveillance and the limitations of interpreting conversations devoid of context. Harry's misinterpretation led him down a guilt-ridden and paranoia-fuelled path, culminating in a shocking twist. The line could be interpreted as 'He'd kill *us* if he got the chance', hinting instead at a sinister plot against the Director.[26] The change in inflection re-contextualises Harry's ethical struggle, amplifying the film's commentary on the pitfalls of surveillance and the propensity for misunderstandings when invading private conversations.

---

26 The film's editor Walter Murch discusses how the inflexion came about in this interview: https://youtu.be/O2RRaw08og8?si=DxIc8h0IIv8VaukM

At the film's conclusion, audiences are left to question the nature of the surveillance industry. If a seasoned professional like Harry can misinterpret a conversation, how much trust can we place in surveillance as a tool for truth? The narrative appears to impart a sobering lesson – that surveillance, in its essence, infringes upon privacy and can lead to disastrous outcomes predicated on misinterpretation.

The twists surrounding the line 'He'd kill us if he had the chance', its change in inflection, and the unexpected conclusion, all contribute to establishing *The Conversation* as a timeless classic. Its examination of the privacy–personalisation paradox is especially relevant in the current era of digital marketing, where businesses are compelled to strike a delicate balance between using consumer data for personalised experiences and respecting privacy rights. The film serves as a stark reminder that breaching this boundary can lead to calamitous consequences.

[**END OF SPOILER**]

The Conversation, with its intricate narrative and moral contemplations, provides more than mere entertainment. It presents a cautionary tale, a commentary on the hazards of surveillance and a clarion call for the respect of privacy in an increasingly interconnected world. It encourages us to question, to understand, and to challenge the status quo in a world where privacy continues to be a precious commodity. Through its intricate narrative and moral contemplations, *The Conversation* transcends mere entertainment, serving as a cautionary tale against the perils of unchecked surveillance. It is a poignant reminder of the delicate balance between the technological advances that promise convenience and the imperative to safeguard our most fundamental rights. As Coppola masterfully illustrates, the echoes of our conversations may carry far beyond their intended reach, leaving us to ponder the true cost of our interconnectedness in our digital age.

Privacy–personalisation Paradox

So, apologies for the Marketing 101, but let's go back to basics and look at the 4 Ps of Marketing – I know we often talk about 7 but I don't have that much space. Did you know that the production costs of a book are directly linked to the number of pages and images?

Product, Price, Promotion and Place

Back to my time working with the four iconic brands in the Natura & Co portfolio at the time.

The beautiful range of products from Natura LATAM. This is marketing.

The great pricing available on Avon International products. This is marketing.

The promotions available to The Body Shop customers. This is marketing.

The beautiful architectural experience of an Aesop Signature Store. This is marketing.

So, all aspects of marketing … but there is one P that we mistrust so much that we have to read pages of legal speak before opting into that aspect of marketing.

We don't read Ts and Cs when we walk into a store – we assume that it has been built with the highest standards of safety in mind.

Yes, we read the ingredients on the back of the product, but to a certain extent we assume that brands don't sell us unsafe products.

And we take it for read that the price we see on that web page is the price we are going to pay at the checkout and is a fair price.

But when it comes to the actual promotion side and receiving marketing messages and the use of our data, we come across an inherent mistrust of brands.

So much so that we have to convince customers to share their data with us and get them to read 10 pages of terms and conditions.

But Data Privacy is important – consumers across the globe place more trust with companies who don't overexert their use of personal data, whether that be asking for more data than is necessary or use the data for purposes other than originally communicated to the consumer.

Note – I refuse to add references that link to statistics that highlight this paradox as:

1 – by the time you read this they will be out of date

2 – you know the gist of the numbers

3 – they were generated by organisations which sell personalisation or privacy capabilities/consultancy services. And they wouldn't publish figures that were detrimental to sales, would they?[27]

But here's the conundrum or privacy v personalisation paradox as it is often described.

---

27   But if you did want to some figures … https://www.cuzziol.com/numbers

Customers do want personalised experiences. And when I talk about personalisation, I don't just mean personalised emails. I mean relevant messaging, tailored user journeys online, being recognised in store, tailor-made subscription offers, a 'Hello Gianfranco' when I walk into my favourite retailer.

And consumers are willing to share data to get that personalisation … the numbers seem to stack behind that idea … and of course we see that personalisation does actually translate into increased revenue – if taken to the right level.

But that sharing of data will only be achieved where there is trust between consumer and brand. Do they trust you enough and see the benefits of taking the red pill to see just how deep the rabbit hole goes?[28]

So, what is Trust? Not wanting to get too philosophical about it, I found these quotes I liked.

> 'Consistency is the true foundation of trust. Either keep your promises or do not make them.'
>
> *Roy T. Bennett*

> 'Do not do what you cannot continue to deliver. For, remember, the world wants to see a continuity of delivery of set standards …!'
>
> *Sujit Lalwani*

Here trust is framed around consistency and keeping promises. Sounds like a brand philosophy to me.

And again, as seen in some of the insights from the Edelman Trust Barometer Report, Trust is key in brand relationships,

---

28   Oh come on, you got that reference, please? https://youtu.be/zE7PKR-jrid4?si=avToVKAXTISd0gfC

with 81% of responders even highlighting personal vulnerability including privacy (I have just realised I have broken my vow of silence on statistics!).

For the record, data privacy policies don't have to be boring.[29]

So how do we begin to frame these ideas of gaining trust and data across the organisation?

At the core it's about ethics. I think it's about raising the game as to how we think about our customers and their data. It's not about the letter of the law, but the spirit of the law. It is about doing the right thing – even though it might raise tensions between the brand and commercial teams.

This is not going to be eBay. Sitting in an ivory tower at group headquarters has to be balanced with the needs of the commercial teams sitting in Brazil, Australia and Europe.

Culture – as we know – eats strategy for breakfast, though personally I like porridge. In the same way that I rolled out a new way of thinking about CRM across Aesop, this is about knocking on internal doors, dropping digital campaigns, converting the mindset internally about what you're trying to deliver.

And then finally. It's about building in controls … or privacy by design if you remember the GDPR mantra. It's about codifying the Ethics and Culture into systems – it's about fighting the customer's corner even when a business unit tells you that they don't want a customer preference centre.

---

29   Just to lighten the mood a little, data privacy and trust doesn't have to be couched in a ten-page legal document nobody reads, as shown here by channel 4: https://vimeo.com/282685116

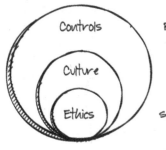

Build controls into your systems & processes

Internal and external : Walk the walk

Spirit of the law, not the letter of the law

Ethics

So, for example, this might all play out when making a decision about the use of third-party data. What's your stance here? How do you educate the business about your point of view, and then build guardrails that control that, for example, by adding into the procurement guidelines?

As you can see, this goes beyond just the conversations we have with customers.

But talking of those conversations:

From a practical perspective, what conversations are you having with customers, where and when?

Perhaps I am a little old fashioned, but I still firmly believe in thinking about growing relationships over time and being mindful of what you are asking on a first, second and third date. Ask the wrong question on the first date and you get a slap on the face. Leave a question until the third date and have you left it too late?

And be very mindful of what the value exchange is perceived to be.

So I talk about Minimum Viable Data (MVD) – which I guess is a data strategy in miniature. Think about the least amount of data you need to collect to solve a customer's need or want and, indeed, to move the relationship on. How much data do you need to offer personalised journeys to your customers?

What's the value to you AND the customer in this value exchange?

Think about how you're going to collect the data ... as this is a factor in determining its quality.

So, in an Aesop store – customers are asked for no more than name and email address. We don't want to ruin the in-store experience – but online a little more can be requested.

Customers are informed why we want their email address. A promise is made not to bombard them with endless promotional messages but to deliver information, or education if you wish, to help them get the most from the products. That promise is kept and they have the highest sign-up rates I have seen ... and some of the lowest opt-out rates!

But be mindful that not all channels provide the same quality of data.

For example, customer's skin type. Which is going to give you a better quality input?

Skin type collected in store after a 40 minute consultation or a pop-up on your homepage asking 'What skin type are you?'

Where do you start when trying to understand MVD?

Well, I guess it really is about the customer ... and understanding them. Their needs, wants and pain points.

I'm a big fan of Customer Journey or Customer Experience Mapping – it really helps to frame these pain points and the opportunities on offer to solve them.

Earlier in this book you've seen an early version of one of Aesop's six-stage customer journeys we developed. And the encouraging thought here is that we pulled this together with without any additional insight requests – we just used the existing customer and consultant insights, profiles and transactional data we already had.

And this evolves over time and plays a key role in determining what data we need and where we should collect it.

I've mentioned previously the term 'cruel optimism' where the object we desire (the new tech on the block) can often be a blocker to achieving what we set out to do.

So, when you are thinking about personalisation, don't think in the first instance about how to crowbar a 'solution' into a problem that didn't exist to start with! Alternatively, think about how personalisation can help a customer fulfil a need or want.

I think there are three key pillars to successful personalisation:

Brand
Trust
Customer

Let's start with brand position, a cornerstone of successful marketing. A brand's position is its unique identity in the marketplace, distinguishing itself from competitors. However, in the pursuit of personalisation, enterprises often grapple with maintaining their brand position while catering to individual preferences. Striking the right balance necessitates a profound understanding that personalisation should enhance rather than overshadow the brand's essence.

Personalisation without Purpose is Pointless

Effective personalisation in marketing should seamlessly align with a brand's core values and promises. By harnessing data and consumer insights, companies can tailor their messaging and offers to cater to the specific needs of their customers, without diluting their brand position. It is crucial to remember that personalisation should serve as a harmonious companion to the brand, fostering a profound connection and engendering unwavering loyalty rather than eroding trust.

At Aesop, much of the content was not necessarily personalised to the individual. Much of the messaging was about culture, the environment and food. These were core tenets of the brand that we wanted to talk about. Emails didn't even have a name personalisation.

But when it came to the welcome journey for a new customer, personalisation was brought to the fore.

The welcome was from the store of purchase, cementing the relationship between customer and the store where they had their Aesopian experience. Content reflected the product purchased with details such as how to use it and suggested complementary products.

The other brands in the portfolio were much more 'tailored' in their communications, reflecting their brand's position in customer minds and indeed their position in the retail high street.

In fact, I've worked with brands which have been guilty of over and under personalisation.

As mentioned previously, I worked with a leading sports broadcaster which had a fantastic breadth of sport on offer. It wanted to personalise its communications not only at sports level, in this case football, but also at club level: Manchester United, Liverpool, Chelsea, etc. Their data and technology gave them the power to do this. We ran the programme with some great content but at a cost. This extra content was expensive and engagement bombed!

What they had forgotten to consider was that the majority of their subscribers had joined because of the breadth of content and sports coverage. If they had wanted club specific content they would have subscribed to the clubs' own TV channels (MUTV, LTV, Chelsea TV) and newsletters.

The marketers had also failed to consider the ultimate flow of KPIs in that the marketing KPIs have to support the business KPIs. One of the KPIs at a corporate was a CSAT-related question that asked if customers were happy with the 'breadth' of sports coverage and content!

So, the marketing team was working against that KPI.

To strike the delicate balance in personalisation, enterprises must prioritise privacy. Transparency must reign supreme with data collection practices and the intended use of the collected data being communicated clearly. Obtaining consent from individuals before acquiring their personal information and affording them control over their data through opt-out mechanisms or privacy settings are integral steps.

Furthermore, integrating privacy by design principles can empower companies to construct privacy-conscious systems from the ground up. By embedding privacy as a fundamental tenet in their marketing strategies, businesses can ensure that personalisation efforts remain respectful, responsible and firmly rooted in legal and ethical considerations.

In fact, where the law ends, ethics begins.

Lastly, we must explore the notion of free will within the realm of personalisation. While tailored marketing can enhance customer experiences and provide relevant recommendations, it is crucial to respect individuals' autonomy. Personalisation should empower rather than manipulate or coerce customers into making decisions.

Best Margin Product v Real Customer Need?

If we can allow customers not to lose the sense of serendipity when discovering new products surely that's a good thing? Part of the strength of Spotify and Netflix is the opportunity to listen to and watch content that may not otherwise have been discovered previously – even if that only happens because the algorithms are not perfect.

To achieve equilibrium, businesses should provide customers with meaningful choices. Transparency and consent hold paramount importance here as well. Granting individuals the ability to control the extent of personalisation they receive and affording options to opt out or modify their preferences is imperative. By endowing customers with the freedom to determine the degree of personalisation they desire, businesses can foster a sense of empowerment and build robust, trust-based relationships.

Finding the delicate balance in personalisation within marketing is an ongoing challenge for businesses. By embracing the fundamental principles of brand position, privacy and free will, companies can successfully navigate this intricate landscape and forge effective personalised experiences for their customers.

Remember, personalisation should elevate the brand's position. Privacy must be prioritised to build trust and maintain ethical practices. Lastly, respecting individuals' free will is paramount to prevent veering into the realm of manipulation.

By embracing these principles, businesses can cultivate personalised marketing experiences that are respectful, pertinent and invaluable. Achieving the right balance allows companies to foster profound connections with their customers and propel sustainable growth in our increasingly personalised world.

And I leave you with one final thought.

Think about data as a prized asset that should be on your balance sheet. Imagine in five years' time that not only does the brand sit on your balance sheet but also your data. Not the quantity of data you have but the quality of that data, perhaps best signified by the level of permissions you have from your customers to use that data and how engaged they are as a result – that's the care and attention it deserves. That's what having customers trusting you and your data strategy can give you.

Nonna's Lasagne Recipe

My mum, Nonna, was famous for her lasagne. Whenever we were back home for the weekend, we would leave with a Tupperware box crammed with several portions.

Her versions varied from the simple to this monster version we had every now and again. It's based on a traditional lasagne served at the beginning of Lent – Lasagne di Carnevale!

There are three main components: The Ragù; The Meatballs; The Lasagne.

Nonna never seemed to follow a recipe so the weights and measures here are a rough guide.

Ragù

1 carrot, diced
1 celery stalk, diced
1 onion, diced
100g Italian sausages
300g pork ribs
125ml red wine (never optional)
1.5kg homemade tomato sauce
2 teaspoons salt
3 tablespoons extra virgin olive oil

Meatballs

200g lean minced beef
60g stale bread
250ml milk
100g freshly grated Parmesan
1 egg
1 teaspoon salt
vegetable oil for frying

Lasagne

300g lasagne sheets

300g ricotta

250g mozzarella (not the posh stuff)

125g freshly grated Parmesan (usually left to me to organise)

2 hard-boiled eggs, shelled.

To create this delicious lasagne, start by preparing the ragù. Begin by dicing the carrot, celery and onion, then stir-fry these with some extra virgin olive oil to make a flavourful sofrito. Into this, add 3 tablespoons of extra virgin olive oil along with the pork ribs and sausage, stirring with a wooden spoon until the meat is seared beautifully. Pour in some red wine and allow it to evaporate, seasoning with salt before adding the tomato sauce. Let the ragù simmer on a low heat for at least 2 hours (preferably 3, which gave us enough time to go to Church on a Sunday morning, sometimes leaving Nonno (my dad) at home working in the garden and occasionally stirring the pot) to develop deep flavours. After simmering, remove the meat from the sauce, setting aside the meat and sausages to use in a second course if desired, and then transfer the ragù into a large bowl to cool.

Next, focus on making the little meatballs. Soak stale bread in milk for an hour, then squeeze out any excess milk. Combine the soaked bread with minced meat, an egg, Parmesan cheese and a pinch of salt, mixing everything together by hand. Shape small pieces of the mixture into meatballs about 1cm in diameter by rolling them in the palms of your hands. Fry these meatballs in some vegetable oil until golden, then remove them from the oil and place on a paper towel to drain off any excess oil.

To assemble the lasagne, start by slicing the hard-boiled eggs very thinly, using an egg slicer for precision (the egg slicer was a later addition to the list of kitchen utensils hidden in the bottom cupboard). Cut the mozzarella into thin slices, using the egg slicer for this as well for consistency. In a bowl, mix some of the ragù with ricotta cheese, loosening the mixture with a fork for easier spreading.

Arrange all your prepared ingredients around the lasagne baking dish. Begin by spreading a layer of ragù on the base of the dish. Place the first layer of pasta sheets over the ragù (depending on your preference, these can be pre-boiled or not. Nonna's method varied). Over the pasta, spread some of the ricotta cheese mixture, followed by an additional layer of ragù. Dot the surface with meatballs and place slices of boiled egg and mozzarella cheese in between them. Sprinkle a generous amount of Parmesan cheese over everything, then cover with another layer of lasagne sheets. Continue this process, building the layers until all the pasta sheets have been used. For the final touch, pour the remaining sauce over the top layer and finish with a sprinkle of Parmesan cheese.

Bake the lasagne in an oven preheated to 180°C for 30–45 minutes. Once done, allow it to cool slightly before serving, letting the flavours meld together beautifully.

IT IS NEVER, EVER SERVED WITH SALAD OR CHIPS!

Alternative Glossary

Behavioural Targeting	Action-Driven Engagement
Bounce Rate	Entry-Exit Resonance
Brand Positioning	Identity Anchoring Strategy
CAC (Customer Acquisition Cost)	Engagement Acquisition Investment
Churn Rate	Attrition Velocity Metric
Competitive Analysis	Market Momentum Mapping
Content Strategy	Informational Engagement Blueprint
Conversion Rate	Action Conversion Quotient
CRM (Customer Relationship Management)	Engagement Coordination Framework
Cross-Channel Consistency	Harmonized Multi-Path Engagement
CTR (Click-Through Rate)	Engagement Navigation Ratio
Customer Data Platform	Customer Information Integration Hub

Customer Database Management	Customer Information Administration
Customer Engagement Platform	Customer Interaction Infrastructure
Customer Experience Management	Customer Interaction Optimization
Customer Feedback Management	Customer Response Coordination
Customer Insight Management	Customer Intelligence Coordination
Customer Interaction Management	Customer Engagement Oversight
Customer Lifecycle Management	Customer Journey Oversight
Customer Relationship Platform	Customer Connectivity Hub
Customer Service Automation	Customer Support Streamlining
Direct Mail	Tangible Touchpoint Messaging
Distribution Strategy	Reach Amplification Plan
E-commerce	Digital Shopping Sphere
Email Marketing	Inbox Engagement Campaigns
Engagement Rate	Interaction Intensity Index
LTV (Lifetime Value)	Relationship Longevity Assessment
Market Segmentation	Consumer Landscape Fragmentation

Marketing Automation	Automated Marketing
Marketing Mix (4Ps: Product, Price, Place, Promotion)	Integrated Value Configuration
Omnichannel	Unified Experience Strategy
Out of Home Advertising	Environmental Brand Displays
Personalisation	Tailored Experience Design
Personalized Content	Custom Crafted Experiences
Platform	Operations Hub
Product Differentiation	Offering Uniqueness Integration
Retail	Physical Purchase Points
Retention Rate	Relationship Sustainability Score
ROI (Return on Investment)	Value Amplification Index
Seamless Experience	Frictionless Interaction Journey
Segmentation	Audience Sculpting of Audience Clustering Framework
Shopping Cart Abandonment	Unfulfilled Basket Syndrome
Social Media	Digital Community Engagement Platform
Social Media Reach	Digital Footprint Expansion

Social Selling	Digital Relationship Sales Strategy
SWOT Analysis	Strategic Terrain Assessment
Target Audience	Focal Consumer Cohort
Unique Selling Proposition (USP)	Brand Distinctiveness Essence

To publish or not to publish?

'Everyone has a book in them, but in most cases that's where it should stay.'

Christopher Hitchens

Please be kinder with your reviews.